Fabulous FRIENDSHIPS

Scrapbooking the Relationships That Make Life Fun

Kitty Foster and Wendy McKeehan

Memory Makers Books
Cincinnati, Ohio
www.mycraftivity.com

About the Authors

Kitty Foster has loved crafts since she was a kid. As soon as she got the big box of crayons (you know, the one with the sharpener in the back), an addiction was born. She was introduced to scrapbooking in 1993 and she has been writing, designing and teaching in the field since 2000. She has been published in many scrapbooking magazines and idea books, and she is part of design teams for several manufacturers. When not scrapbooking, you can find her taking photographs, drinking coffee or coloring outside the lines with one of her kid's crayons.

Wendy McKeehan was brought into the scrapbooking world by a very dear family friend in 1999 and has stayed there every since. One of the things that really keeps her in the business is the amazing friendships she has fostered all over the world. After teaching, demoing and working tradeshows, she is now content to write books and design projects for both traditional and digital manufacturers. When she is not dabbling in ink or playing with pixels, you can find her singing in the church choir, taxiing her favorite scrapbook subjects to various activities or kicking back on the couch with her husband, a glass red wine and a movie.

12 11 10 09 08   5 4 3 2 1

Distributed in Canada by Fraser Direct
100 Armstrong Avenue
Georgetown, ON, Canada L7G 5S4
Tel: (905) 877-4411
Distributed in the U.K. and Europe by David & Charles
Brunel House, Newton Abbot, Devon, TQ12 4PU, England
Tel: (+44) 1626 323200, Fax: (+44) 1626 323319
E-mail: postmaster@davidandcharles.co.uk
Distributed in Australia by Capricorn Link
P.O. Box 704, S. Windsor, NSW 2756 Australia
Tel: (02) 4577-3555

Library of Congress Cataloging-in-Publication Data
Foster, Kitty
  Fabulous friendships : scrapbooking the relationships that make life fun /
Kitty Foster and Wendy McKeehan. -- 1st ed.
     p. cm.
  Includes index.
  ISBN 978-1-59963-022-9 (alk. paper)
  1. Photograph albums. 2. Scrapbooks. 3. Friendship in art. I. McKeehan, Wendy II. Title.
  TR501.F67 2008
  745.593--dc22

                 2008014045

F+W PUBLICATIONS, INC.

www.fwpublications.com

Editor: Amy Glander
Designer: Corrie Schaffeld
Art Coordinator: Eileen Aber
Production Coordinator: Matt Wagner
Photographer: Christine Polomsky
Illustrators: Kristi C Smith and Aruna Rangarajan
                    Anderson Design Group

Metric Conversion Chart

to convert	to	multiply by
Inches	Centimeters	2.54
Centimeters	Inches	0.4
Feet	Centimeters	30.5
Centimeters	Feet	0.03
Yards	Meters	0.9
Meters	Yards	1.1
Sq. Inches	Sq. Centimeters	6.45
Sq. Centimeters	Sq. Inches	0.16
Sq. Feet	Sq. Meters	0.09
Sq. Meters	Sq. Feet	10.8
Sq. Yards	Sq. Meters	0.8
Sq. Meters	Sq. Yards	1.2
Pounds	Kilograms	0.45
Kilograms	Pounds	2.2
Ounces	Grams	28.3
Grams	Ounces	0.035

We dedicate this book to:

To my God: There is no greater love than the one who lays his life down for a friend. Thank you for calling me friend. Doug: How blessed of a woman am I to have a husband who understands my need for girlfriends. Your encouragement means the most. Hannah: I'm so happy that you have learned that girlfriends come first. Thanks for keeping me young. I delight in you. Mom: I watched my whole life as you knew how to enjoy life with your friends. From having an ice cream fight or just having goofy impromptu behavior—I loved it all! Penny: You were my first friend, my mentor and only sister. We share sweet secrets, life goals and DNA! (Mike and Tim like you the best.)

I also dedicate this book to my friends. Mona: Thank you for teaching me how to stick up for myself. You taught me what it meant to have girl power! Traci: It was you who showed me the importance of girlfriend time. How now brown cow! Shannan: I know that you worked in a sportswear department, even though you never played sports and that you would rather die than to eat a hot dog. I know your bra size, your computer password and your real hair color. Thank you for always giving me fitly spoken words when needed. They are apples of gold in a setting of silver. Wendy: You are not only my co-author but my friend. You are a wonderful wife and mom, great friend and the prettiest wallflower that I know. You inspire me. Silvia: You have the ability to laugh at yourself and that soon has me laughing along with you. You're an excellent cook, the funniest little gnome that I know and can swipe a luggage cart in a single bound! Kathe: From the moment we met we have shared laughs, scrapbook supplies and double vision! Our time together can be as deep as encouraging each other over a pickle free zone or just hanging out with Neal while waiting for a good print. It's all good!

-Kitty

All the friends I have known along the way. You have made me who I am today, and I am so grateful. To my first friend and sister Nikki. You have been there the longest, made me laugh the hardest and helped me to grow into the person I am today. It's an honor to share the family nose with you. To my neighborhood friends Nick, Doug, Diane, Todd and Marina. Thank you for kickball games in the street, roller skating and teaching me to swear in Spanish. To my school friends Sima, Ila, Jill and Anj. You all made high school bearable. To my husband Chris whom I met in college. You were then and will always be my best friend. To my church friends Nancy, Jami, Margaret, Dianne, Jen, the girls of the Spirited Women Bible study and the Chancel Choir. You are all such wonderful blessings in my life. To my scrapbook friends Kitty, Steph, Stef, Debi, Jes, The DD CT, Kelly E. and Sharyn. You have all shared your friendship, laughter, opinions and expertise with me, and I am forever grateful. Keep scrappin' the good stuff!

-Wendy

Acknowledgments

We are grateful to the following companies for their generous donations: 7Gypsies, Autumn Leaves, Crate Paper, Daisy D's, DesignerDigitals.com, Fancy Pants Designs, Hambly Screen Prints, Inque Boutique, Masterpiece Studios, Scrapbook Adhesives by 3L™ and WorldWin Cardstock.

We were blessed with an amazing pool of contributing artists to round out this book. Thank you all for trusting us with your scrapbook pages and sharing your stories of friendship. It is our honor to include them in this book.

Special thanks goes out to Christine Doyle for running with another book idea of ours and Eileen Aber for her mad organizational skills. You both are the best!

Table of Contents

Chapter **Four**

Chapter **Five**

Neighbors by Kitty Foster
Supplies: Patterned paper, stickers, transparency (Creative Imaginations); buttons (Autumn Leaves); adhesive (3L); Misc: Times New Roman font, ink

She lives in Chicago and I'm in Atlanta, but when we

finally get to see each other, it seems like we are neighbors!

We were sharing a hotel room at the Craft and Hobby Association trade show in Chicago when I looked at the counter and realized that we used the same deodorant (although different scents) and that's when I knew that what we had was more than a friendship...it was a sure thing!

A Sure Thing by Wendy McKeehan
Supplies: Digital brushes and papers by Anna Aspnes (Designer Digitals); template by Kellie Mize (Designer Digitals); embellishments, overlays by Katie Pertiet (Designer Digitals); Misc: Century Gothic and Impacted fonts

YOU GOTTA HAVE
Friends

Friends help you move. Real friends help you move bodies.

—Author Unknown

According to our trusty source the dictionary, friendship is defined in this manner:

Friendship \friend•ship\ n. 1. a relationship between two or more people who are friends 2. the mutual feelings of trust and affection and the behavior that typify relationships between friends 3. a relationship between individuals, organizations or countries that is characterized by mutual assistance, approval and support.

While the definition here is valid, it makes one small omission. It doesn't mention the years a friendship endures, the laughter heard when good friends are together, or the understanding and comfort only a true friend can offer. The dictionary, we're afraid, cannot begin to define the word.

Friendship is one of the biggest blessings a person can experience. Our friends are there when all is well, but they can also motivate us when we're ready to throw in the towel. They help us find our inner strength and also have a way of keeping us grounded. We often just want them around to have a good time, to laugh or to enjoy a mutual activity like scrapbooking. Friendships are willed or chosen—we aren't dragged into them kicking and screaming. They aren't like being stuck in a boring meeting, a traffic jam or a long line going nowhere. We are there because we want to be.

A natural progression for those of us who love to record our memories is to make sure we include our friends in the pages of our albums. Many of us consider our friends to be like family, and it should follow that these relationships play a prominent role in our scrapbooks. You can have a page about your favorite aunt right next to one about your girl's night out with your best friends from high school. It's all a part of who we are—every great bit of it and our scrapbooks can affirm this. *Fabulous Friendships* is the book to help you include friendships of all varieties in your scrapbooks. This book is a celebration of friendship—it is good for your heart, good for your soul and, well, good for scrapbook ideas!

The best mirror is an old friend.
— George Herbert

Chapter one
HOW IT ALL Began

Sometimes you meet someone and you and she just click. Fast friends, both in the sense that you hit it off quickly and that you've created a bond that won't easily break. Whether that person is from the house down the street, someone you met on the first day of school, or a kindred spirit that you met later in life, these "classic" friends are just like classic songs or movies—you turn to them time and again for comfort, support and to remember special times. Now is the time to look at these relationships and record the fond memories that make friendship so sweet. These classic friendships are a great trip down memory lane and a fun way to remind our own children that we were once kids, too.

Childhood Chums

Hit the rewind button and go back in time—back to a time before the Internet, computer games or cell phones. A sweet time when things were simple and innocent, and the biggest hardship in friendship was trying to figure out who would be the banker in Monopoly. These were the friends who knew our deepest secrets like where we kept our allowance, our bra size and whom we had crushes on. Childhood friendships are the ones that have shaped us into who we are today and give us the ability to connect our past with our present.

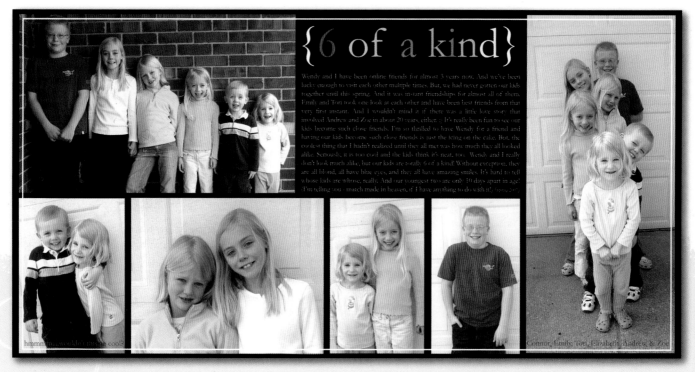

Artwork created by Stephanie Vetne

Stephanie and Wendy lined up all their kids nice and pretty in a row for an impromptu photo shoot only to realize that all six kids look a lot alike (even though they're from two different families!). Look for coincidences and curiosities as you flip through your photos. You may be surprised at what strikes you. In this digital layout, Stephanie kept it clean and simple with a collage of photos accented with a colorful title and a single paragraph of journaling telling the amusing story of these six little friends.

Supplies: Software (Adobe); Misc: Garamond font

Wyatt, Kent, and Kurt met the Murphy boys before Kent and Kurt were even in Kindergarten. The Murphys were friends-of-friends of ours and when the Murphys finally moved into our neighborhood, Brenden, Kent, and Kurt became fast friends. As chance would have it, Brenden had an older brother, Ryan, who was in the same grade as Wyatt. They too hit it off from the beginning. They all became inseparable.

So now, on the first day of school, Wyatt, Kent, and Kurt can be seen walking with their best friends. First grade and fifth grade. A little nervous, maybe. But on this first day of a new year, friends make it easier...entering a new grade, with a new teacher. Friends give them confidence and reassurance. Friends make an anxious day a positive day. Being with friends starts the new year off right.

First Day

Artwork created by Mary Larson

Friends give confidence and reassurance. Friends make an anxious day a positive day. Being with friends starts the new year off right. Could it be said any better? Use your journaling to not only tell the story of a common event among friends, but to also share pearls of wisdom that apply to both childhood and grown-up friendships. Pull colors from your photos for a cohesive design and use a strip of rickrack or ribbon to draw the eye to the focal photo on the page.

Supplies: Cardstock (WorldWin); patterned paper (Crate Paper, Daisy D's, Stemma); adhesive (3L); Misc: ink, rickrack

you &

SHE

You and she have been the best of friends since before you were born. You came into this world 16 days apart and Dorothea and I just knew you would adore each other. We were right! From being stroller buddies to crawling after one another, you've always had a big smile when she was around. 'Jordan' was even one of your first words. Now, as toddlers you're running, climbing and laughing together! Your special friendship is so sweet. As the years go by, I hope that you'll always remain as close as you are now.

Artwork created by Anabelle O'Malley

This boy-meets-girl page tells the story of how these two little tykes, born only a few days apart, became the best of friends. Anabelle is excited to see how their relationship will evolve as they grow older, but she wanted to chronicle their friendship just as it is now in the sweet years of toddlerhood. Use chipboard letters, torn edges and velvet-embossed paper to add a cozy, textural feel. For a quick and easy floral accent, trim flowers from patterned paper and add a colorful rub-on image to the centers.

Supplies: Cardstock; patterned paper (Crate Paper, Making Memories); chipboard letters (Li'l Davis); letter stickers (BasicGrey); rub-ons, tag (My Mind's Eye); Misc: Bookman Old Style font, paint

Artwork created by Kim Moreno

Living on a military base has its challenges and making good friends is certainly one of them. Brandon didn't become friends with just one of the Moreno kids—he became friends with all five! Kim created this layout to honor this young man's special place in their family. Use geometric prints such as stripes, polka dots and concentric circles to add movement and energy to your design, as Kim did here.

Supplies: Cardstock; chipboard letters, patterned paper (Scenic Route); rub-on letters (Making Memories); photo corners (American Crafts)

Artwork created by Stephanie Vetne

These girls have been neighbors since birth and friends since they both can remember. Stephanie documents their special friendship in this digital layout with four portraits and an array of swirls and flourishes. Use your scrapbooks as a way to pay tribute to one or more friends who have had an impact on your life or to commemorate a milestone they are about to experience.

Supplies: Digital flower embellishments, frame, patterned paper by Tia Bennett (Two Peas in a Bucket); text paper (artist's own design); Misc: Lainie Day font

Ideas for Featuring Fabulous Friends

Here's a list of ideas to get you thinking about the different types of pages you can create to honor your friends in your scrapbooks.

* How you came to be friends
* Qualities you admire most in your friend
* How your friends would describe you
* Common interests
* Biggest differences

* What your friendships have taught you
* Special acts of friendship
* Ritual get-togethers and getaways
* Favored ways of keeping in touch
* Greatest moments shared

how long

Through chili on retainers and lipstick on letters, through 90s hair, straight hair, and badly permed hair, through ugly boyfriends, abusive boyfriends and no boyfriends at all, through tears of laughter and tears of pain, through drunken nights and nights holding babies tight, through new boobs and saggy ones, through marriages and almost divorces, through celebrations and lonely times, through hot pants and fat clothes, through road trips and camp outs, not just through the good times and the bad, but all the moments in between

1990

no way

SERIOUSLY

How long?? Really, I can hardly keep track. You've been in my life longer than not. We were 13 when we met and barely 14 when this photo was taken in a photo booth at Fun Spot. I know you loathe this picture, but I cherish it. It reminds me of our beginning and all the things we been through.

Artwork created by Creasa Brown

Creasa selected this endearing middle school photo of herself and her best friend beaming with sweet smiles and tender-hearted dispositions. Attach a chipboard accent like this butterfly to add whimsy and a girlish charm. Use a primary color palette of red, yellow, blue and green and journal on notebook-style paper trimmed into strips. Adhere the journaling strips to the bottom border to ground your page.

Supplies: Patterned paper (American Crafts, KI Memories, My Mind's Eye, Sassafras Lass, Scenic Route); letter stickers (Doodlebug, KI Memories); chipboard (AccuCut, Heidi Swapp, Making Memories); date stamp, labels (Making Memories); buttons (Blumenthal); brads (Queen & Co.); Misc: floss

Friendship Memorabilia

We all have collected mementos, souvenirs, letters or clippings over the years of our oldest and dearest friendships. Consider using them to add meaning to your layouts. If the originals are too large or precious to adhere right on your layout, simply make yourself a color copy and scale it to fit your needs. Don't forget to include:

* Ticket stubs from concerts or events you've attended together

* Friendship charms

* Printouts of e-mail correspondence

* Notes passed in class

* Greeting cards

* The song list from a mixed CD of favorite songs

* A relevant journal entry

Artwork created by Deena Wuest

Deena scanned notes and memorabilia from her fun-filled high school days with her friend Jenny. Ticket stubs, handwritten notes and photographs all unite to make this digital page an authentic memoir of this teenage friendship. Collect memorabilia from your school days and scan it as Deena did here, or include originals directly on your page.

Supplies: Software (Adobe); digital bulletin board by Kellie Mize (Designer Digitals); fasteners, journaling accents, photo frame, tags by Katie Pertiet (Designer Digitals); letter clips by Leora Sanford (Little Dreamer); Misc: Avant Garde and Impact fonts

old Friends   My Girls   Best Friends

10 Year Reunion   {i love these girls}

These girls I have known since preschool — some
since birth.
I've laughed with them. I've cried with them. I've loved
with them. I've lost with them.
I can talk to them about anything.
I doesn't matter how long it's been since we have seen
each other. We still carry on as if no time has passed.
28 years of friendship is a priceless thing to have and
I'm sure there are many more to come.
I love you all.
I love these girls.

Artwork created by April Massad

April has been friends with some of "her girls" since preschool and knows she is blessed to have each and every one of them in her life today. Creating a layout like this is easy using your computer. Simply create your design using Microsoft Word or another word-processing program, and then print it onto a solid sheet of cardstock. Trim various color or black-and-white photos, and adhere them side by side atop a strip of patterned paper for a quick and easy photo filmstrip.

Supplies: Cardstock; patterned paper (Scenic Route); stamps (Autumn Leaves, Technique Tuesday); Misc: CK Jacque font, ink

Then and Now

The bond that you've created with a childhood chum is one to be cherished, and sometimes, if you're lucky, it turns into a lifetime bond. These friendships endure even as our lives change tremendously, through high school, onto college and perhaps even into when you get married and start having kids of your own. Creating scrapbook layouts of these friendships is too much fun—to record the evolution of a friendship and to show off some pretty crazy hairstyles.

then

I met Traci in 8th grade at Reed Jr. High and I always thought she was funny. In High school we were in a 9th grade electives class, speech & debate with Mrs. Carter and we had a complete blast. Somehow, Mrs. Carter found us amusing and we passed with flying colors. That same year, we both tried out for drill team. I made it she didn't. The next year, I was determined that she would. I was her "big sister" and worked her to death and she made it. The next two years in drill team were so much fun. We both had several other friends but would still laugh all the time together. In the fall of 1987, a year after high school, we connected again. We both were coming out of relationships and just needed a girl friend, and that we were. We spent tons of time together and laughing harder than I ever thought possible. We both met our husbands that summer and got to see the beginning of the relationships bloom. We called each other after engagements, went shopping for wedding attire and eventually even worked together. She was in my wedding but I wasn't in hers. Immaturity on my part caused a dumb grudge and we had a simple but not angry falling out. I regret that so. During my visit to Texas to see my parents in the summer of 2007, we were able to see each other again. We met at a restaurant and got to spend some time with each other but not enough. We talked and talk and finally had to leave the restaurant - so we chatted another hour in the car! We have stayed in touch through email and a few phone calls since then. Traci will always be a sweet friend and hold an important part of my past and future.

and now

Artwork created by Kitty Foster

Kitty and Traci have that special kind of friendship where no matter how many miles separate them, whenever they see each other they can always pick up right where they left off. A friendship like this deserves a special place in your album. Use a bold color palette to make a big statement, as Kitty did here with her combination of pink, orange and green papers and floral accents. Convert color photos to black and white to keep them cohesive and use a font that mimics handwriting to keep it easy yet personal.

Supplies: Cardstock (WorldWin); patterned paper (Autumn Leaves); stamps (Inque Boutique); adhesive (3L); Misc: 2Peas International font, ink

In the summer of 1976, my family moved from a quiet barren neighborhood to one that was filled with kids. I was thrilled but was even happier when I soon discovered that there was a girl next door. Bonus! Mona was a year older than me so this made her all the more alluring. She played with the older cool girls in the neighborhood and I was sometimes lucky to tag along. She was funny, had great hair and was very secure in herself. She was everything I wasn't. As the years went on, we became closer. I was her biggest fan when she tried out for 8th grade cheerleader, her greatest confidant and if a guy broke her heart, I plotted revenge. Then came the worst thing that could possibly happen — I was told we were moving. I was devastated. So, the summer of 1981, my family moved to another city and I was forced to find new friends. Mona and I kept in touch and visited each other every summer and we always managed to pick up where we left off. It was during one of these summer visits, that we both bought this best friends key chain with our initials on the back. I wonder if she still has hers. Years went on and we both grew up. I was in her wedding and was thrilled to bring my new fiance', Doug to meet her. It was the beginning of a new life for the both of us. Mona is such a part of who I am today — she taught me about defending myself when we fought, social tips and unconditional friendship. I just wish I knew where she was now.

THE GiRL NEXT DOOR

Artwork created by Kitty Foster

In this layout Kitty journals the story of her friendship with "the girl next door." Almost all of us have had friendships that started simply because of the street we grew up on. Add a row of buttons and painted chipboard letters to give a bold punch of color to black-and-white photos. In the lower right corner, you'll see Kitty included half of a friendship key chain. These types of trinkets and treasures serve as a great visual accent while adding sentimental value to the story you're telling on your page.

Supplies: Buttons, chipboard letters, patterned paper, ribbons (Daisy D's); adhesive (3L); Misc: Blueprint font

IDK, my BFF Jill?

Friday, June 08, 2007
Current mood: ecstatic
You know, you've seen it..... that annoying cell phone bill commercial where the little pre-teen brat talks to her mother as if she's texting:
Mom: Who were you talking to?
Brat: I D K? My BFF, Jill? (I don't know? My best friend forever, Jill)*
Ironically, Mom seems to understand what is being said because in the end, she tells her daughter, "My paying this bill is what's "SNF." (so not fair)*
Much as I hated the commercial at first, eventually it really just makes me laugh. I realized my generation didn't have texting (Hell, we didn't have cell phones. Some of us were the s*** simply because we had a phone in our bedrooms!) Instead, we had notes. Yes, we passed NOTES..... in class, between class, on the bus, after school. This was how we communicated when "live-and-in-person" was impossible. But what happens when you can't pass notes anymore? What if you don't know where to send the note? A ha... and so technology and the internet save the day!
I had a "BFF Jill." She was the most amazing person I knew. I could count on her no matter what. Every secret was shared with her. Every decision was made with her input... in true junior high – high school fashion! We had nearly identical class schedules throughout most of high school. Every weekend was spent hanging out or on the phone. I'm sure most of us had a true blue friend like this. She was mine. Even into college and into our first marriages we remained close friends. There's nothing quite like being able to have a conversation without having to retell the previous 10 years of history. She just "got it." It was also nice to have someone tell you the truth. Not just what you wanted to hear. ("No girl, it's your A**.that makes those pants look big. NOT the other way around!") She had no problem knocking me off my pedestal when I got too high and mighty (which happened more times than I care to remember).
If it's possible to be enamored of a friend, I was of her. She was pretty and funny and smart. Everyone liked her – EVERYONE. She was always kind to everyone she met. Regardless of clique, she would speak to you. The cheerleaders, the stoners, the band geeks – she fit in everywhere. I wanted so much to be like her. I was just thankful she was my closest friend. Sure, we both had lots of other friends. We both had interests that didn't include the other. But no matter what, me and her – BFF.
Alas, life is what happens when you're busy making plans. People get older; lives change. We drifted apart. Years passed. Now, almost a decade later, I still thought of her. A lot. I wondered where she was, what she was doing. I wondered if she realized what a tremendous impact she had on me as a human being. I wondered if she knew how much I missed having her in my life.
I'm happy to say I finally found my BFF. (Ok, more accurately, she found me.) Quite by accident, as it usually happens, but I'm thrilled nonetheless. Most likely we won't be "passing notes" as often as we once did. Lives, husbands, children, and careers all take up most of our time now. That's okay. Even if we only manage an email from time to time or a Christmas card with the family newsletter once a year, it's really okay. I know where my BFF is.... no more I D K.

Artwork created by Christy O'Bryant

Christy and her friend Jill first became close during years of note passing, hanging out and talking on the phone. In this journaling-intensive layout, Christy used modern cell-phone "speak" to depict their relationship then and now. This is an interesting way to chronicle what's popular or mainstream in a particular time period. In decades to come, she may look back and say, "Oh, yeah, remember when we used to talk like that?" Inject these pop culture references into your layouts as a sort of time capsule to preserve these cultural tidbits.

Supplies: Cardstock; patterned paper (BasicGrey); letter stickers (Scenic Route); acrylic hearts (Heidi Swapp)

Thirty five years! That's how long Missey and I have been friends. It's so hard to believe that is even possible until I look back on our lives together. Missey and her family moved into our neighborhood when we were both five years old. I remember running home to tell my mom that I had a new friend. We were inseparable for literally years after that. She and I, along with Sandi and Mary, did EVERYTHING together - walking to school, playing in the park, riding bikes, playing house, Barbies, trick-or-treating, ice skating, making up gymnastics routines on the swing set, sleepovers, birthday parties, boat rides, rollerskating, growing up, getting our hearts broken by boys, graduating from high school, being bridesmaids in each others weddings, baby-sitting each others children, and most recently, being there when parents were ill and dying. I feel so blessed to have her in my life and look forward to seeing what the next 35 years brings to our lives.

Artwork created by Vicki Harvey

Vicki's friendship with Missey has spanned more than three decades. To illustrate the progression of time, Vicki used photographs from three different stages of life—middle school, high school and "all grown-up." Then-and-now layouts can be a lot of fun to create if you have photos from different periods of life, whether the theme be friendship, changing clothes and hairstyles, "all-about-me" or something else entirely. Include additional elements, like the clock accent on Vicki's layout, to further suggest the passage of time.

Supplies: Patterned paper (Mustard Moon); chipboard letters (BasicGrey); clock accent (Li'l Davis); digital notepad sheet by Tia Bennett (Two Peas in a Bucket); Misc: Falling Leaves font, flower, paint, thread

It Started at Hello

That classic friendship doesn't always start in childhood, however. Sometimes even as adults we strike it rich with a chance meeting that turns into an enduring friendship. Record these relationships in your scrapbooks, too, for before you know it, you'll be ready to scrap "then and now" layouts about these friends as well.

we did. we just clicked. it started with polite getting-to-know you conversation but about 30 min after i met her it became real. and it just got better from there. she is such a beautiful person inside & out and im so glad i got to meet her... 10/29/06

Photo: Kelly Miller

Artwork created by Cheryl Manz

From the moment they met, Cheryl and her friend Kelly "clicked." She tells the story of their first encounter in simple handwritten journaling. The beauty of this page is in its simplicity. To achieve a clean look like Cheryl's, adhere a stunning black-and-white photo of you and a friend atop a sheet of crisp white cardstock. Add paper flowers with felt and button centers for a punch of fresh color and apply letter stickers for an easy title.

Supplies: Cardstock; patterned paper (Scenic Route); brads, letter stickers (American Crafts); buttons (Autumn Leaves); Misc: flowers, pen

Artwork created by Liana Suwandi

One day when Liana's friend's little boy mistook her for his mom, Liana knew they were alike in more ways than she realized. To honor this special friendship and look back on how it began, Liana created a page full of layers. To add some texture, melt a crayon in a melting pot and dab the colored wax around the page to created dots or other design elements. This is an easy and inexpensive way to add bursts of color to a page. For extra sparkle, apply glitter glue on hand-cut elements.

Supplies: Cardstock; patterned paper (Scenic Route); chipboard letters and accents (Chatterbox, Die Cuts with a View, Fancy Pants); die-cut shapes (Daisy D's, Sizzix); ribbon (Die Cuts with a View); rub-ons (BasicGrey, Chatterbox, Deja Views, Die Cuts with a View, Me & My Big Ideas, My Mind's Eye); stickers (7gypsies, EK Success); stamp (7gypsies); Misc: Impact font, decorative punch, ink

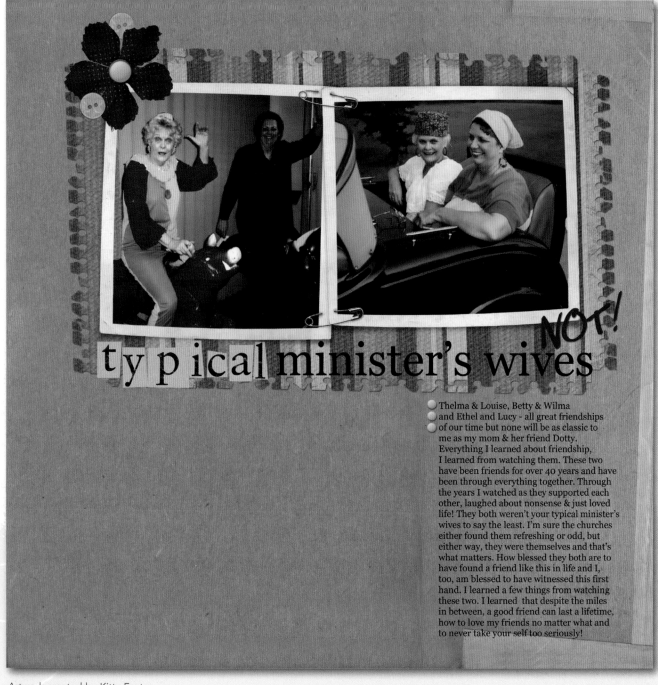

ty p i cal minister's wives NOT!

Thelma & Louise, Betty & Wilma and Ethel and Lucy - all great friendships of our time but none will be as classic to me as my mom & her friend Dotty. Everything I learned about friendship, I learned from watching them. These two have been friends for over 40 years and have been through everything together. Through the years I watched as they supported each other, laughed about nonsense & just loved life! They both weren't your typical minister's wives to say the least. I'm sure the churches either found them refreshing or odd, but either way, they were themselves and that's what matters. How blessed they both are to have found a friend like this in life and I, too, am blessed to have witnessed this first hand. I learned a few things from watching these two. I learned that despite the miles in between, a good friend can last a lifetime, how to love my friends no matter what and to never take your self too seriously!

Artwork created by Kitty Foster

This is an ode to a wonderful partnership. Kitty credits her Mom and Dotty for really teaching her the meaning of a great friendship. So this page is dedicated to a couple of wild and crazy girls! Kitty allows the photos to really pop by accenting them with the single flower and button embellishment and by leaving plenty of white space on the page.

Supplies: Digital papers by Dana Zarling (Designer Digitals); frame, Kraft paper, title letters by Katie Pertiet (Designer Digitals); flowers by Lynn Greiveson (Designer Digitals); brads by Anna Aspnes (Designer Digitals); buttons by Pattie Knox (Designer Digitals); Misc: Especial Kay and Georgia fonts

Artwork created by Paola López-Araiza Osante

Paola used childhood photos of her dear friends for this page. Even though they didn't know each other when they were kids, they are all quite sure they would have gotten along as well as they do now. This proves you can still make fun "then-and-now" layouts featuring childhood photos even if you didn't know each other way back when. It's a great way to show a side of a friend you may not have seen before. You can use a traditional sepia color palette, or go bold by adding a punch of color with orange, blue or green, as Paola did here.

Supplies: Patterned paper (7gypsies, BasicGrey); chipboard letters (Heidi Swapp); ribbon (Autumn Leaves, Making Memories, Rusty Pickle); stamps (Sassafras Lass); buttons (Autumn Leaves); Misc: ink

No good thing is pleasant without friends to share it.

—Seneca

Chapter Two
SO Happy TOGETHER

Let's face it—everyone loves to have a good time. We all want to get together with our buddies to kick back, laugh and make some great memories. This is the quintessential definition of friendship. When we are asked to describe our best friend, many of us launch into the retelling of the craziest things we did with our friends, what they do to make us laugh or the mad adventure we shared "back in the day." It is a natural extension that those moments end up on our scrapbook pages. We would wager that some of the easiest scrapbook pages to design are centered on the theme of "fun with friends." These pages usually have fun colors, engaging photos and, of course, good stories. Turn the page for some fresh and fun examples.

Girls Just Wanna Have Fun

Cyndi Lauper was right—girls really do wanna have fun! From giggle-filled slumber parties to meeting up with the gals from the Red Hat Society, we all enjoy the company of our gal pals. Girlfriends of all ages enjoy the moments that bring bountiful smiles and contagious laughter. So whether it's a princess tea party, a bachelorette weekend or just sitting in the waves at the beach laughing at nothing in particular, record these special moments in your scrapbooks. They are sure to make for a great read later.

Artwork created by Kitty Foster

This layout features the quintessential friendship shots in the photo booth. And, yes, tongues are required. Scrapbooks are the best place to feature silly smiles and funny facial expressions. So if you don't already have pictures like this in your photo box, find the closest mall, festival or theme park and snap away! Enlarge one photo as a focal point and accent it with jazzy patterned paper for an eye-popping page.

Supplies: Cardstock (WorldWin); patterned paper (American Crafts, Creative Imaginations); adhesive (3L); Misc: Arial and Times New Roman fonts, pen

Artwork created by Staci Etheridge

Staci and Shonnery rediscovered their love of dance while shopping at Target and decided to bust a move right then and there while strolling down the main aisle. Don't be afraid to capture the silly side of a friendship. Perhaps you have a friend who puts you in stitches whenever you're together. Archive these fun times in your scrapbooks so that years later when you flip through your albums, you can relive the moment (and have a hearty laugh while you're at it). For extra fun, create your title from a play on words, as Staci did here.

Supplies: Patterned paper, stickers (KI Memories); chipboard letters (Heidi Swapp); sticker accents (7gypsies); chipboard accent (Imagination Project); buttons (Autumn Leaves, Doodlebug); labels (Dymo); digital label by Tia Bennett (Two Peas in a Bucket); Misc: rhinestones

strong invincible WOMEN

Eight gorgeous girls. Smart. Diverse. Connected. We call ourselves the GTO, and once a month we set aside time to bond. Beth and I hosted the August meeting on the first Friday of the school year by setting up a fitness session with Amanda at Pine Ridge. With energizing music and challenging but fun exercises we worked up a sweat in no time! Our trip for ice cream afterwards was well deserved.

Mollie, Susan, Monica, Jessica, Jenn, Beth, Tanya, and J'Nelle   8.25.06

Artwork created by Susan Opel

Aerobics and ice cream—now that's girl power! Do you have a club, group or special set of friends you see perhaps once a week or once a month? Whether it be a book club, bowling league or prayer group, celebrate these friendships forged from a common interest. Susan pays homage to this special group of women with an oversized photo complemented with fun and funky patterned papers. For a bold title, use large and colorful lettering like she did to really pack a punch.

Supplies: Cardstock; chipboard flowers, patterned paper (KI Memories); Misc: Agency FB, Bernard MT Condensed, Century Gothic and Engravers MT fonts, brads

They met because their Mom's are friends and now they can't imagine their lives without each other. Tori and Emily write emails and letters almost daily. It is worth the 2 hour drive to get them together to play every once and awhile if for nothing else than to get them to pose for the camera!

strike a POSE

Artwork created by Wendy McKeehan

Thanks to their moms' Internet friendship, Emily and Tori became fast friends, too. It can be interesting to chronicle the similarities, or differences, between little-girl friendship and grown-up friendship. Do little girls gab as much as their moms do? Can they spend as many hours at play as their moms spend scrapbooking? Start looking for the parallel attributes that distinguish these bonds. Choose a colorful palette to match your subjects' personalities, as Wendy did here to convey the exuberance of these two little friends.

Supplies: Patterned paper (Fancy Pants); chipboard letters (Crate Paper); stamps (Inque Boutique); adhesive (3L); Misc: ink

Artwork created by Lisa Tutman-Oglesby

Lisa loves to watch her daughter Cameron chitchat with her girlfriends on the phone. Her journaling documents her amazement that girls of this young, tender age can have so much to talk about. Is there an aspect of your daughter's friendships that fills you with wonder or disbelief? Or perhaps simply makes you laugh? Record these impressions in your scrapbooks so that as your daughter ages you can note the changes and the constants.

Supplies: Cardstock; patterned paper (Chatterbox); chipboard brackets and letters (BasicGrey); flowers (K&Co.); rub-ons (Urban Lily); rhinestone accents (Heidi Swapp); Misc: transparency

Page-Friendly Photos

Composing strong photographs is easy if you follow a few basic principles. By working with the visual elements around you and allowing yourself to see creatively through the lens, you can compose pictures with fresh, unique perspectives. Here are a few basic tips to get you started:

Keep it simple
Eliminate busy backgrounds by avoiding bright objects, busy patterns and other distracting elements.

Get everyone to pose
Group photographs are definitely a challenge! If possible, avoid lining everyone up in a row. Instead, arrange your photo subjects in a staggered line, sideways line or triangle cluster. These arrangements formed by people of varying heights will add visual interest and warmth to a photo.

Follow the rule of thirds
When looking through your lens, divide the frame into thirds, both horizontally and vertically, and position the important elements along those lines.

Be creative
Try different angles by kneeling down, getting low or looking up. A diagonal tilt of the camera will convey a sense of speed, movement or action.

Artwork created by Jen Erickson

This girl's night out proved to be therapeutic as well as informative! Jen passed along a clever photo tip to her gals in Scrap-a-latte for striking the perfect pose. Keep it simple by adhering word stickers to describe fun qualities of your group and use a journaling pen to directly write the names of your photo subjects onto the photo if you're looking for a quick and easy alternative to computer-generated journaling.

Supplies: Patterned paper, chipboard accents, stickers (Imagination Project); chipboard letters (Heidi Swapp); letter stamps (EK Success); Misc: ink, notebook paper, pen

Artwork created by Staci Etheridge

As if scrapbook conventions aren't fun enough, these two can find silly ways to entertain themselves no matter where they go. Staci created this 8½" x 11" (22cm x 28cm) page to chronicle all the fun and laughter of meeting up with a friend for this annual retreat. Use bullet-style journaling to list items, ideas or feelings that sum up the theme of your page. Letter stickers, labels and chipboard letters make creating typography a breeze, and staples are a fun way to adhere gathered ribbon to your page.

Supplies: Cardstock; chipboard letters and shape, patterned paper (Scenic Route); letter stickers (Chatterbox); buttons (Autumn Leaves); labels (Dymo); stamps (Provo Craft); Misc: paint, staples

The
3 OF US
together
graduation   weddings   travels
laughter   tears   joy
and, I know there is more to come.
C L & A

Artwork created by Amelia McIvor

Amelia has been blessed with not one but two great friends. She captures a wealth of good times spent together in a photo collage she created using image-editing software. This is a fabulous and easy way to arrange a variety of photos without the tedium of using scissors and glue. Shake things up a bit by hand stitching an image or swirl using a piece of patterned paper as a template. Use simple words or phrases for journaling to keep your text short and to the point.

Supplies: Patterned paper (BasicGrey, My Mind's Eye, Scenic Route); letter stickers (Adornit); chipboard (Heidi Swapp); Misc: circle punch, floss, pen

Artwork created by Julie Fei-Fan Balzer

Julie learned the hard way that getting a group of women to cooperate for a picture was much more challenging than she thought. Sometimes the photos that may not seem "picture perfect" at first glance can be the most revealing. Put these not-so-stellar pics to good use by lining them up across the top and bottom borders of a two-page spread. Put the winning photo in the bottom right corner and call attention to it with a frame or mat. Let loose by adding humorous handwritten commentary directly to the photos.

Supplies: Cardstock; letter stickers (Deflect-O); stickers (7gypsies); Misc: pen

Artwork created by Sandi Minchuk

Sandi feels that she and her friend Kim are so connected that they not only share the same sense of humor but the same brain. Do you have a word, phrase or inside joke known only to you and your best friend? Share it with the world on a scrapbook page. Years to come you will find it interesting to see how language and phrases evolve, and what may once have been a part of your regular vocabulary may be replaced with something just as quirky.

Supplies: Cardstock; patterned paper (BasicGrey, My Mind's Eye); letter stickers (BasicGrey, Making Memories); die-cut letters (BasicGrey); buttons (My Mind's Eye); Misc: My Own Topher font, brads, floss

Artwork created by Lisa Risser

Playing pretend has been a favorite pastime of little girls for centuries. These two pretended to be the princesses they really are as they danced and twirled about this famous estate. To illustrate their special friendship, Lisa used rich hues and textures to complement her striking photos. Capture a silly, spontaneous or imaginative activity shared between young friends. Over time it's easy to forget the simple things that once brought us great joy. If they are recorded in our scrapbooks, they stay alive in our memory.

Supplies: Patterned paper, brads, dimensional stickers (K&Co.); chipboard letters (American Crafts, Heidi Swapp, K&Co.); chipboard heart (Li'l Davis); ribbon (K&Co., My Mind's Eye); Misc: Baskerville Old Face font, paint

hey sister,

Christine and I aren't sisters!!!!
by birth, but we were definitely
sisters in another life. We
are best friends and have
been since the day we met.
Now that we are both married
and live 2,000 miles apart,
we don't get to see one another
as often as we'd like, but it
doesn't matter how far apart
we are, we are linked for
life. We even showed up to
an event with the
exact same
purse!

Soul
sister

Artwork created by Kory Anne Dordea

Kory discovered that when it comes to fashion, great minds really do think alike. Do you have a handbag, outfit, pair of shoes or other accessory that a close friend also calls her own? Document the coincidence in a scrapbook page! Add a polka-dot silk flower or strips of ribbon to create movement and energy on the page. If you go for fresh and bright colors, use a vivid palette of pink, orange and green with a touch of black for a little sophistication.

Supplies: Cardstock; patterned paper (Autumn Leaves); letter stickers (Reminisce); rub-ons (Doodlebug); flower (Petaloo); ribbon (May Arts); Misc: buttons, staples

SHARING the **DAY**

June 2007 and the Kiwipeas get together for a weekend at Sunset Drive.
Between us we would have taken hundreds of photos that weekend. This out of focus, random action shot
is my favourite though. It sums it all up in one picture.

Lucy pouring a drink, Kathleen hanging out at the bench talking, camera bag sitting in front of her,
Tania cleaning up while Tana and Kate print photos for a scrapbooking project we are all doing.

Artwork created by Nic Howard

There were hundreds of photos snapped between this group of New Zealand scrapbookers during their weekend retreat, but Nic chose this random, out-of-focus action shot because it captured who they really are. Sometimes the best shots are the candid ones that show us just being ourselves. Layer and stitch a garden of patterned papers and add a scalloped border like Nic did for a soft, feminine feel.

Supplies: Cardstock; patterned paper (Scenic Route); letter stickers (Adornit, Scenic Route); chipboard letters (CherryArte); ribbon (Fancy Pants); rub-ons (Autumn Leaves, Daisy D's); Misc: My Own Topher font, ink

Artwork created by Kitty Foster

On a whim, Kitty decided to enter a friendship essay contest for a magazine and to her shock she won the grand prize—a five-day trip to New York City with her best friend Shannan. She shares the details of their adventure in this travel mini album. Mini albums are great for displaying photos and memorabilia of a girlfriend getaway. You'll find the album format gives more room than a typical 12" x 12" (30cm x 30cm) layout, yet the pages are small enough so you won't feel compelled to overfill them.

Supplies: Chipboard album (Maya Road); decorative tape, patterned paper, ribbon, stickers (7gypsies); stamps (Inque Boutique); metal letters (American Crafts); adhesive (3L)

Sisters to the Scrapbook

Scrapbook supplies need not be reserved for run-of-the-mill 12" x 12" (30cm x 30cm) layouts. Use your artistic prowess to get crafty to create adorable gifts and keepsakes that step beyond the page. There are all sorts of ideas for unique gifts and keepsakes you can bestow to a special friend.

- Cards
- Mini albums
- Doorhangers
- Clipboard or decorative dry-erase boards
- Photo frames
- Photo boxes

Artwork created by Kimber McGray

Good times can come in the form of participation in a beloved hobby. On this layout, Kimber shares the story of how she passed the sewing bug onto her young friend Jordan. Use notions or other craft supplies to support the theme of your layout, as Kimber did here with buttons, fabric, machine-stitching and a background created from an actual sewing pattern. Include close-up shots of the project you are featuring to illustrate detail.

Supplies: Cardstock (WorldWin); patterned paper (Jenni Bowlin, Mustard Moon); title letters (Scrapworks); buttons (Autumn Leaves); adhesive (3L); Misc: floss, ink

she is the meredith to my izzie

* live * enjoy * grow * shine * adventure * en

conversation

KA: we need a twisted sister!
S: we already have one! me!
KA: like, meredith grey dark and twisty?
S: yes! that's me! i'm good w it!

fashionista

Artwork created by Kayla Aimee Terrell

There have been many TV friendships through the years—Lucy and Ethel, Mary and Rhoda, Meredith and Izzie. This *Grey's Anatomy*-inspired layout commemorates Kayla's fun, quirky friendship, as well as one of her favorite TV shows. Find fun or silly things in today's pop culture to include in your layouts so they are still rich in your memory in years to come. Make use of white space by keeping a portion of your layout empty so the focus remains on the photo and journaling.

Supplies: Cardstock; patterned paper (American Crafts, Provo Craft, Scenic Route); letter stickers, rub-on border (American Crafts); paint stickers (Adrienne Looman); stamps (Hero Arts); digital swirl by Rhonna Farrer (Two Peas in a Bucket); Misc: glitter, ink, pen, transparency

For the Boys

Girls do not have the monopoly on having fun. Let us not forget the guys in our lives as well. Our boys have their weekly golf outings, monthly happy hours at their favorite bar and other hobbies and activities that keep them on the go. These relationships and events should be recorded and added to our scrapbooks right alongside our girlfriend adventures.

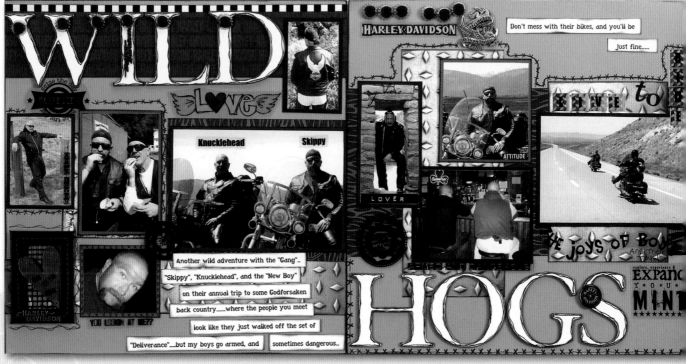

Artwork created by Kary Lewis

We could all learn something from Skippy and Knucklehead—especially how to let go, be free and look good in chaps. In this Harley-inspired layout, Kary shows how her man lets off a little steam by hitting the road with his best biker bud. Choose papers and embellishments that support your theme and have fun adding doodles and other textual elements to lend a rugged, masculine feel.

Supplies: Cardstock; metal embellishments, patterned paper, stickers (EK Success); chipboard letters (Making Memories); chipboard heart (Heidi Swapp); digital kit (Two Peas in a Bucket); Misc: ink, transparency

making your own
good times
that's what you boys do. I'm not gonna lie - I was a little confused when I drove into the court and you boys were running around dressed like this. I should have known you were making another movie. It's what you've been doing all summer. you, connor, and Dave have been friends forever and when you add a few others like Brad, and Brad to the mix, a mom just doesn't know what will ensue. You are crazy goofy funnier than I can believe and full of ideas to keep yourselves busy! I love that you are such great friends after all these years! glad you can make the good times happen!

Artwork created by Laura Fiore

When you're a teen, sometimes life can be a little dull and you are forced to make your own fun. Laura captured these shots of her son and his friends "in character" as they acted out their first feature film. Should they someday become famous, these will be the "before" shots the paparazzi will kill for, but in the meantime Laura puts them to good use in her scrapbooks. Does your teen make his or her own good fun with friends? Describe their friendship and their antics on a scrapbook page. Add geometric shapes like stars and circles for a youthful flair.

Supplies: Cardstock; letter and bracket stickers, patterned paper (KI Memories); chipboard (Magistical Memories); transparency (Hambly); rub-ons (Fancy Pants); Misc: ink

Text within the artwork:

4th Grade Field Trip to see "Bunnicula"

wingmen of MaYhEM

October, 2006

Friends since 4 year old Kindergarten, Josh Wegner + McCoy can bicker like Jack Lemmon and Walter Matthau in "Grumpy Old Men." (Thanks for the analogy, Mr. Jones!) But with shared interests in Star Wars and video games, these two nuts have a real boyhood bond.

Artwork created by Katie Swanson

Mayhem follows Josh and his best bud McCoy everywhere they go. Katie depicts the bond between these two boys in this visually packed layout. Action shots and candids are some of the most fun photos to include in albums so grab your camera and snap away. Use arrows to draw the eye to your photo subjects and keep the background clean of too many embellishments by including only a few lines of simple handwritten journaling and narrow strips of patterned paper to the top and bottom borders.

Supplies: Cardstock; patterned paper (Arctic Frog); chipboard letters (Heidi Swapp); letter stickers (Me & My Big Ideas)

explore

Aaahh! The thrill of a good session of windsurfing ... lots of wind, plenty of waves - the higher the better you guys always say - and good buddies to share it all with. You've been known

ENJOY THE JOURNEY
PERFECT
Explorers
EXPEDITION
exotic
destinations
nature
PLAYGROUND
RAIN OR SHINE
EXPLORING
discover
adventure
ENJOY
GETAWAYS
travelers
BORN TO EXPLORE
OUTDOOR
SCENIC
EXCURSION
By Sea
ESCAPE
Destination
getaways

WINDSURFING

ADVENTURES

Artwork created by Paola Lōpez-Araiza Osante

This friendship started out with the love of windsurfing, but ended up being so much more. Do you have a hobby or passion that connects you with a group of people who share a common interest? In this example, Paola used a clear transparency background and acrylic letters to support her wind and water theme. Try using an array of word stickers to share details about an adventure in a quick and easy way.

Supplies: Patterned paper and transparency (Hambly); title letters (Heidi Swapp); chipboard embellishments (KI Memories); journaling cards (Jenni Bowlin); ribbon (Fancy Pants); stickers (Making Memories); Misc: clip, thread

Group Therapy

For those of us who have a better half, some of the most cherished memories are the activities, events and surprises we share with our spouses and like-minded friends. It could be a neighborhood dinner club that has met for years, a group of lifelong friends that makes an annual trek to a lake house, or a team of parents who have spent countless hours on the bleachers rooting for their kids on the football field or basketball court. These are some of the most easiest and most fun relationships to chronicle in our scrapbooks.

Artwork created by Cindy Tobey

You may be surprised at how much fun a date night without the kids—but with plenty of fish—can actually be. Cindy shows what a great time both couples had on this outdoor adventure on Lake Michigan in this two-page spread. Think back to a unique outing or experience shared with another couple and record the fun that ensued on a scrapbook page. Search for everyday household items to support your theme as Cindy did here with a mesh produce bag to mimic a fisherman's net. Frame some of your photos in circles for a fresh appeal.

Supplies: Cardstock; chipboard letters and accents, patterned paper, ribbon, rub-ons (Fancy Pants); letter stickers (EK Success); Misc: Futura Book font, ink, paint, staples

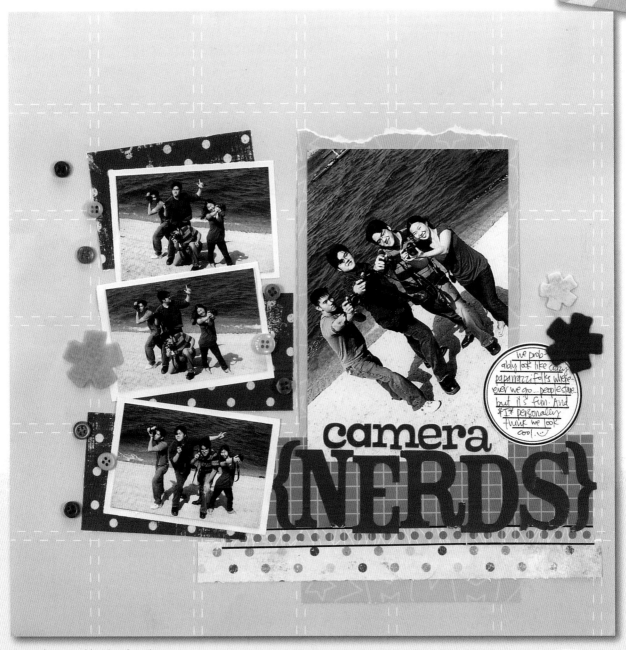

Artwork created by Caroline Ikeji

When Caroline and her photography-lovin' friends get together, there's never a shortage of fun (or memory cards). Come out from behind the camera to include yourself in group shots and experiment with unique angles and perspectives. Mat supporting photos onto gray or white cardstock to achieve a retro "Polaroid" feel. Adhere buttons and felt accents for a little dimension and texture.

Supplies: Patterned paper (Daisy D's, KI Memories, Stemma); felt, letter stickers (American Crafts); journaling tag (One Bored Girl); decorative tape (Stemma); adhesive (3L); Misc: buttons

Meeting Lucy was literally a bit of luck. She found out about me when someone left a comment on her blog asking her if she knew about my blog since we both live in Lyon. After leaving comments on each others' blogs for a few weeks we finally met and became fast friends. But even better our husbands have a lot in common too and so we get to-gether as a foursome quite often!

Good food
Good wine
Good times

life's simple pleasures   life's simple pleasures   life's simple pleasures

Artwork created by Francine Clouden

Sometimes we are lucky enough to meet our online friends in person. Here, Francine used handwritten journaling to tell the story of her and her husband enjoying a good meal and red wine with their newfound Internet friends. For dinner party or food-themed pages, don't forget to include a mouth-watering close-up shot of the cuisine. Repeat a simple quote along a strip of paper, and add fanciful rub-on swirls for a bit of whimsy and soft charm.

Supplies: Patterned paper (BasicGrey, Scenic Route); letter stickers (Making Memories, Scenic Route); tag stickers (Making Memories); rub-ons (Hambly); Misc: paper punches

The one thing I don't mind sharing with my husband is my friends. It's so great that when we all get together, we all laugh, talk and share our friendship as well as good jokes!

Bill and his girls - 2007 -

- 2007 -

Shared Circle

Artwork created by Kimber McGray

What's mine is yours and what's yours is mine. That's certainly the philosophy in Kimber's household where her husband shares a bond with her friends as well. The patterned paper, an oversized chipboard circle, mini brads, and a circular tilt of the title all support the friendship theme on this clean layout. Find a shape or pattern to symbolize your topic and play it up by repeating these elements throughout the page.

Supplies: Cardstock (WorldWin); patterned paper (Polar Bear Press); chipboard letters (Heidi Swapp); chipboard accent (Scrap Supply); adhesive (3L); Misc: brads, ink

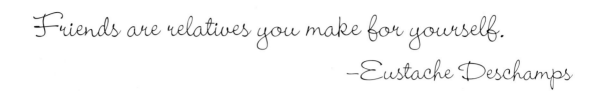

Friends are relatives you make for yourself.
—Eustache Deschamps

Chapter Three

NON-TRADITIONALLY
Yours

This chapter covers the more unusual friendships: friends of different ages, members of the opposite sex, Internet friends, pals who have nothing in common and even your relationship with God. These are the unique relationships that help us grow to become more well-rounded individuals. Maybe for you it's a group of older women from church who offer support or a sincere friendship with a professor who impacted your life. Whatever the case, these friends are an important part of your journey, and we'll show you several examples of how to record their stories to get you started.

Cyber Friendship

The Internet has opened us up to a whole new way to meet and stay in touch with friends. No longer are we bound by proximity or history. Now many of us have wonderful friendships that span the globe based on common interests (scrapbooking, cooking, pregnancy, photography, coin collecting, etc.). The instant gratification of e-mail keeps us all in touch easily, and some tech-savvy folks can even video e-mail one another to show off a new hairstyle, a completed project or just to make funny faces into a camera!

Artwork created by Gretchen McElveen

Gretchen loves to chat with her many Internet friends on message boards, but decided she would much rather spend time with them IRL (in real life). She got the opportunity when they decided to meet up at an annual scrapbook convention. If you have a collection of photos from a single event, create a collage of mini photos onto a graph paper background. Add handwritten journaling for a personal touch and use words or phrases unique to your topic. Here, Gretchen included popular Internet abbreviations and lingo to support her cyberspace theme.

Supplies: Patterned paper (Creative Imaginations, KI Memories, Scenic Route); small letter stickers (EK Success); rhinestone accents (Heidi Swapp); bookplate (Junkitz); Misc: mailbox letters

we've been through a lot together
and most of it was your fault....

what if I had never met Amy? Well, one thing is for sure: I would never have found a friend that makes me feel so comfortable in my own skin that I can just be myself around her and I know she'll love me anyway. Although we're hundreds of miles apart, our minds and our opinions on topics just click as if we were neighbors. We've shared secrets, ideas, gossip, and even a bed! But my hope is that I get to share many more years with her as my friend. Besides, no one can make me laugh with a text like Amy!

what if...

a friend is like a good bra; hard to find, close to your heart & supportive

HOT CHICKS   BEST FRIENDS   YOU & ME

Artwork created by Alexis Hardy

Can't imagine your life without your e-mail buddy? Neither could Alexis so she scrapped a page to remind herself of this special friendship. She used image-editing software to create a mini montage of photos that resembles the traditional photo booth set of photos. To keep a friendship layout like this quick and easy, use handwritten journaling and add fun iconic images such as a cell phone and airplane to symbolize a long-distance friendship.

Supplies: Cardstock; patterned paper (Dream Street, KI Memories); letter stickers (Dream Street); rub-ons (BasicGrey); stamp (Sassafras Lass); chipboard accent (Fancy Pants); stickers (7gypsies); Misc: ink

"An amazing woman and talented artist. Inspiring in every sense of the word. Witty, fun and down-right brilliant. Yep, that's Becky."

deena

connected

"Deena. Full of humor. Full of grace. I can't remember when or how I met her, I'm just glad I did. Deena. A mentor. A teacher. A friend."

becky

I've never met her in person...never even heard her voice. So how is it that we're friends? Well, I guess you could say we share a passion. A passion for creating art, a passion for family, a passion for life. We scrapbook, and in doing so we get a glimpse into each other's lives. The good, the bad, the triumphs and the struggles. Through sharing our honest emotions, we are connected...even across 769 miles.

Artwork created by Deena Wuest

With a little help from Becky, her featured subject, Deena crafted a stunning digital layout that illustrates a friendship that spans many miles...769, to be exact. The map pattern was the perfect choice to support her theme, and the dots serve as a great way to visually express the long-distance connection. Brainstorm creative ways to communicate a thought or idea in a visual way. Look to magazines, print ads or even children's books for inspiration. Another fun technique is to add cartoon-style quotes next to each photo subject.

Supplies: Software (Adobe); digital paper by Katie Pertiet (Designer Digitals); brushes by Anna Aspnes (Designer Digitals); bubble thoughts by MaryAnn Wise (Designer Digitals); Misc: Interstate Light font

Artwork created by Cheryl Manz

It took a wedding for Cheryl and Courtney to finally meet in person after three years of friendship via e-mail and phone. Sometimes a single word like "Finally" is all it takes to sum up a story that's years in the making. Cheryl told details of their long-awaited first encounter in the handwritten journaling wrapped around a patterned paper circle. The arc of the circle draws the eye downward to the paper flowers accented with a rainbow of colorful buttons. Keep it simple by including one stellar photo that will pop on a solid black background like this one.

Supplies: Cardstock; letter stickers, patterned paper (Scenic Route); flowers (Prima, Scenic Route); buttons (Autumn Leaves)

A Different Kind of Friendship

Who says a friend needs to be someone your own age, your own gender or even a "someone" at all? While they may not be traditional, these friendships may be enduring ones or they may be extremely meaningful at a particular time in our life. Either way, scrapbooking these relationships will record their importance in your life.

Our lives are very different. Our ages span over four decades. Yet we find much in common through our love of all things creative. We request a table for three, usually at Too Bizarre. We get together for lunch just to share our projects, ooh and aah over each others creations and offer advice and constructive criticism when needed. We catch up on family stories and news of other friends. We enjoy being together at our little table for three.

Artwork created by Amy Tara Koeppel

This is a wonderful layout documenting a great luncheon tradition between three women from three different decades. Not only is this a great story to record, it is a great reminder of the gift of friendships with people who are in a different stage of life. This layout shows there is so much we can learn from each other and our experiences. If you're featuring three photo subjects, repeat photos and accents in threes like Amy did here.

Supplies: Cardstock; die-cut shapes, patterned paper (BasicGrey); flowers (Petaloo); number sticker (American Crafts); Misc: Kartikan font, eyelets, ink, transparency

Artwork created by Caroline Ikeji

Caroline shares a fond memory of an older neighbor whom she visited often as a child. Although her friend is no longer with us, she has a special place in Caroline's heart for being such a great friend when she was a little girl. Documenting a nontraditional friendship like this is important because as time goes on our memories fade. The photos and journaling on your scrapbook pages will always serve as a tangible reminder of how a special friend touched your life.

Supplies: Cardstock (WorldWin); patterned paper (American Crafts); letter stickers (Heidi Grace); stickers (Heidi Grace, KI Memories); tag (7gypsies); flower (Queen & Co.); rhinestones (Target); adhesive (3L)

like family

FAVORITES BEST MOST GREATEST TOO MUCH NOT ENOUGH JUST RIGHT

LOVE AND BE LOVED REMEMBER ATTEMPT REAL LIFE FACTS WISDOM

I have known Nico for almost ten years now. We met just a few days after my husband and I got together. He is my husband's best friend and he has been since they were teens. We instantly clicked and we often did things with the three of us. When our first child was born he was there with a huge present and held him tightly. Right that minute "Uncle Nico" was born. My husband and Nico got the same tattoo, a Chinese word that means family. One year he went on a vacation with us to Italy and we had such a good time there. Nico is just always there for us whenever we need him, always there without a doubt. He doesn't ask for much, he is kind of the silent guy, sweet and with a big heart. Whenever my husband makes fun of me Nico is always there to stand up for me, taking my side. So even though he is my husband's best friend, he also holds a special place in my heart.

HOPE CREATE LAUGH OUT LOUD REACH OUT SERVE OTHERS BE KIND

Artwork created by Corinne Delis

Corinne wanted to express how she feels about her husband's best friend Nico, who has also become a close friend of hers over the years. The title perfectly sums up how she feels about him and his place in their lives. Place an image such as a circle or transparency over a photo subject's profile to highlight him or her. Distress part of the photo for a dramatic effect and adhere foam stickers to create an easy title.

Supplies: Cardstock; patterned paper (American Crafts, Hambly); patterned transparency (Hambly); letter stickers (American Crafts); stickers (7gypsies); Misc: Times New Roman font, staples

WHEN EVER

You are always here for me.
You are my best friend, my hope.
You never let me down. I can
always read your wonderful
words of encouragement, whenever I need too. You rejoice
with me. You weep with me.
My life is complete in you. I owe
my life to you. You are my healer,
my hand holder, my strength.
I thank You, Jesus... I love you.

Artwork created by Andrea Wiebe

Andrea considers God to be one of her closest friends, and her Bible is a special part of that relationship. Do you have a special book that draws you in again and again? Or perhaps you have a precious memento, keepsake or heirloom from a relative or friend. Whatever it may be, photograph it and share its meaning on a scrapbook page. Over time those items may rust and fade, but scrapbooks can create an everlasting record of those items you hold most dear.

Supplies: Cardstock; patterned paper (Making Memories, unknown); flowers (American Crafts); buttons (Doodlebug); Misc: ink, letter stickers

Artwork created by Julie Geiger

When in the depths of a personal trial, Julie discovered God was her best friend, and she created this layout to honor this personal relationship. Her heartfelt journaling is honest and sincere and shares her hope that others will discover the joy and comfort she has found in walking the path of faith. Include mini photos as Julie did here to showcase others who are a part of your life. Trim paper hearts and flowers as accents to convey a sense of joy.

Supplies: Cardstock; patterned paper, stickers (KI Memories); stamps (Paper Trunk); paper tagger (Around the Block); ribbon (Heidi Swapp); rhinestone accents (Making Memories); Misc: ink

Somewhere in that double bed is a boy... a boy who adores his stuffed animals, each with a name. Lyon the lion has been with Kyle since he was born. I used to sing him to sleep with the lyrics of "In the Jungle", with Lyon dancing and howling up a storm. Torteese comes from our good friends, Marv and Carol, a Christmas gift to their adopted grandchild. A most recent addition is Elling, a true-to-life safari elephant. Santa searched high and low to find such realism in a stuffed animal.

But did I say "stuffed"? I apologize. Of course these animals "feel pain", so I must be careful not to sit on them when I come in to pray at night. These animals have personalities, and are allies in war games. Once in a while they accompany Kyle to school, and often they listen intently while he reads. So yes, somewhere in that bed is my boy... reminding me very much of a little girl from about 30 years ago... lying in a bed surrounded by fuzz and fur, unable to sleep without the companionship of...

LYON

TORTEESE

ELLING

bed budzzz

Artwork created by Rita Shimniok

Sometimes friends come in the soft and plushy variety. Most of us can relate to a bed filled with beloved stuffed animals. Rita's son has sought his animals out for comfort, as war allies when he plays games and as reading partners. What a great childhood memory to document. Use stripes, circles, stars, arrows or other geometric shapes to create movement and energy on a colorful page like this one.

Supplies: Cardstock; patterned paper (Scenic Route); chipboard letters (Queen & Co.); letter stickers (Scenic Route); chipboard frame (Magistical Memories); Misc: Jester font, paint

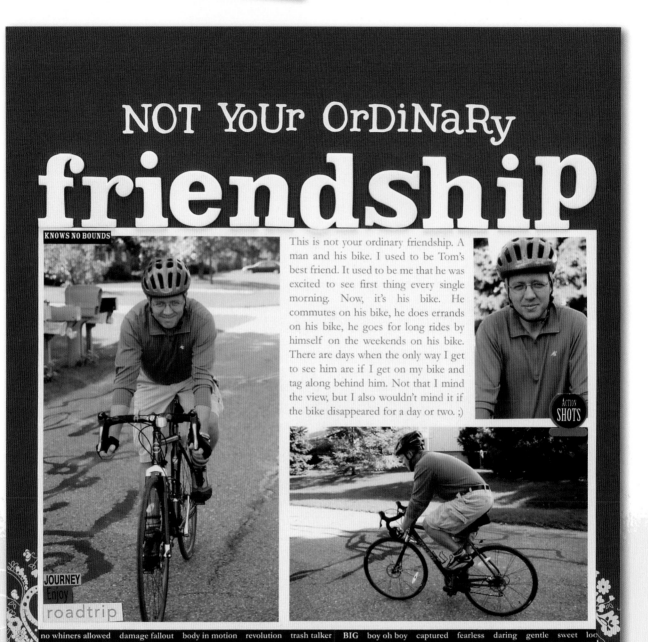

NOT YOUR ORDINARY
friendship

KNOWS NO BOUNDS

This is not your ordinary friendship. A man and his bike. I used to be Tom's best friend. It used to be me that he was excited to see first thing every single morning. Now, it's his bike. He commutes on his bike, he does errands on his bike, he goes for long rides by himself on the weekends on his bike. There are days when the only way I get to see him are if I get on my bike and tag along behind him. Not that I mind the view, but I also wouldn't mind it if the bike disappeared for a day or two. ;)

ACTION SHOTS

JOURNEY
Enjoy
roadtrip

no whiners allowed   damage fallout   body in motion   revolution   trash talker   **BIG**   boy oh boy   captured   fearless   daring   gentle   sweet   loo

Artwork created by Stephanie Vetne

On this page, Stephanie documents her husband's love affair with his bike. Do you have an item in your life that is not only purposeful for the obvious reasons, but also serves as a great source of enjoyment? Perhaps it's a camera, cell phone, iPod or even a soft and fluffy sweater. Whatever it may be, document its importance in your scrapbooks because someday you may come to fall in love with something else, and the memory of your cherished items may fade with time.

Supplies: Cardstock (WorldWin); letter stickers (American Crafts, Doodlebug); stickers (7gypsies, Making Memories); rub-ons (BasicGrey); adhesive (3L); Misc: Garamond font

My Own Best Friend

One thing we have to realize is that acceptance can only come from within and will take place over time if worked on. We have to increase our self-love and respect as much as we can—even if only in small increments. We have to do this until we know deep within our beings that we are smart, beautiful and worthy of respect. What better way to start doing this than to scrapbook the ways in which we are our very own best friends?

I am loyal, trustworthy and I believe in myself. Problem — in a society filled with women who are insecure, I sometimes feel that I should apologize for this. I should only be sorry if I have done something wrong and the fact that I know that I have something to offer, deserve respect and have an overall love for life is certainly nothing to apologize for. If someone around me is insecure about themselves, I am compassionate but I will not shrink. I refuse to. If I shrink down with them — what has that proven? I have gained this inner strength from trudging through years of insecurities but found that besides God, I am my true best friend. When others left or betrayed me, I was the only one who could pick up the pieces. It was hard at times, but I did it and I'm glad. I am a strong woman and I make no apologies for it.

No apologies

Artwork created by Kitty Foster

Kitty scrapbooks her marriage, her parents and countless pages about her children. but rarely does she scrapbook a page about herself. Sound familiar? She realized the pages she wants her children to see the most are the ones that share her strong beliefs. She wants them to know there is so much more to her than carpools, bad dinners or being a referee. So she pulled out her journaling pen and let the feelings flow. Her children will appreciate her sentiments both now and in the future and will have an everlasting keepsake of what was important to their mom.

Supplies: Patterned paper (Creative Imaginations); adhesive (3L); Misc: Times New Roman font

This is not an easy time in your life in many ways. Kids can be cruel. Sometimes it is intentional and sometimes it is not but either way it is a painful process to watch you go through. I know it is all part of growing up. We all had to suffer through middle school pettiness and meanness but that doesn't make it any easier to watch you deal with it.

But here's the thing. You are handling it pretty well. Sure, you get upset when kids say mean things to you. Yes, you storm off and cry. But when you calm down you understand a little bit more about yourself. And you seem to be creating a strong sense of self acceptance. I have to admit, I did not have that when I was your age and it still throws me to see you gain strength in your convictions and move on from the pettiness. You are getting it.

You asked a kid the other day why he's so mean to you and another friend at practice, but then calls the other friend to play after such mean remarks but doesn't call you. He informed you that he "hated you". I asked you if you were upset by this, and you replied, "Mom, he's a nitwit." See, you get it. You are learning that the words while a bit painful initially, do not define you. You have struggled with this in the past which is why I'm even more impressed with your new found self confidence.

My fervent wish for you is that this trend continues. I know the kids will still be mean and hurtful, I just hope your convictions remain strong and that you stay on your path of confidence and self worth. You are really starting to know yourself and that is amazing. As your Mom, I know my opinion does not count in the relative scheme of things, but I am so very proud of you and how you are growing up. I wish I could claim credit for it, but I truly believe that you have found this strength from within. Keep on this path Connor and all the good that life has to offer will be yours for the taking.

October 2007

KNOW THYSELF

Artwork created by Wendy McKeehan

Growing up is a time of self-acceptance and discovery. If you can begin to know yourself in the early years, your personal friendships with others will be much stronger as you grow older. In this digital layout, Wendy wrote a letter to her son so he would know his self-acceptance was beginning and what a great thing that was to watch unfold. Letter writing is a great way to express your deepest and most heartfelt feelings to a loved one. Let the journaling flow and don't be afraid to hold anything back.

Supplies: Digital distressed edge, overlay, paper, title letters by Anna Aspnes (Designer Digitals); grunge overlay by Katie Pertiet (Designer Digitals)

Is it hard to make new friends?

I have been asked this question many times throughout the past 13 years and each and every time, my answer is "yes."

It can be extremely difficult to make new friends when you're the wife of a military man. Trying to make a whole new set of friends every 3-4 years is no easy task, but it's one that I find I'm getting better at.

And when they ask me who my best friend is, who the greatest friend I have made throughout these past years is, I just smile and say me.

I am my own best friend.

I love myself unconditionally and am proud of my accomplishments. I can rely on myself and I don't have to worry about being hurt or letting myself down. I know what's important and what's best for me.

Some may wonder if it's lonely having yourself as your own best friend and I say OF COURSE NOT! if you can't be a best friend to yourself, if you can't put faith and trust in yourself, then how can you be those things for others, or expect others to be those things for you?

Artwork created by Mandy Koontz

In this digital layout, Mandy shares her optimistic view on her current situation. Being married to a military man she has learned that although friendships with others are important, ultimately, she is her own best friend. Use your scrapbooks as a place to share your perspectives on relationships for both yourself and others. Not only will you reaffirm to yourself the importance of your self-acceptance, you may also offer insight to someone else going through a similar experience. Allow yourself plenty of room for journaling and highlight your portrait with a frame and ribbon accents.

Supplies: Digital background paper by Heidi Williams and Saxon Holt (Weeds and Wildflowers); cardboard overlay by Linda Gil Billdal (ScrapArtist); black flowers, frames, mini ribbons, paint splats (Christina Renee); circle brushes by Michelle Coleman (Little Dreamer); ribbons (Christina Renee, Shabby Princess); buttons (Shabby Princess); funky flowers by Annie Manning (Oscraps); Misc: Pea Kelly font

PERFECT by imperfect

I can very distinctly remember myself at age 13. Looking at the women in magazines and always wondering why I couldn't be perfect like them. I felt like I was the only girl in the world struggling with self image. I was tall, had more than my fair share of pimples, and to top it all off, I had naturally curly hair that wouldn't cooperate if my life depended on it. There were days I couldn't even look at myself in the mirror. Fast forward 20 years. I'm still tall, I still struggle with those darn pimples, and that hair? You guessed it ... still here and still defiant. Oh, and you might as well throw 20 pounds, wrinkles and gray hairs into the mix! So what's different? Somewhere along the way, my heart changed. I don't quite know when it happened, but I learned to accept myself. I learned to love myself. I realized that God purposely formed each part of me. Purposely! And in that moment, I realized that I *am* perfect. Perfect in the eyes of God. Imperfections and all! 09.2007

Artwork created by Deena Wuest

Growing pains aren't just physical, as many of us have experienced. Deena struggled with self acceptance for many years. Now, years later, many things about her physically have changed, but the big change has come in her understanding of her self worth. She shares the story of that evolution in this digital layout, in which she wraps the journaling around her photo to further highlight the body she has come to accept.

Supplies: Software (Adobe); page kit by Katie Pertiet (Designer Digitals); paper collection by Anna Aspnes (Designer Digitals); Misc: Avant Garde, Steelfish and Susie's Hand fonts

Artwork created by Julie Geiger

On this layout, Julie expresses that after going through many trials, she finally discovered who she really was and that she could be her own best friend. This portrait taken by her daughter only shows half of her face, but she felt it was particularly befitting for a page sharing these thoughts about how far she has come in her journey of self-discovery. Use symbolic images to support your theme as Julie did here with photos of an angel and a cross to represent her faith.

Supplies: Cardstock; border stamps, patterned paper (Paper Trunk); chipboard letters (American Crafts); journaling tags (7gypsies); stickers (Creative Imaginations); fabric tab (Imagination Project); flower accents (Making Memories); jeweled brad (SEI); Misc: decorative scissors, ink

I have this crazy love/ hate relationship with myself, although most of the time, it's in the "hate" category. Why is it so much easier to be your own worst enemy, and put yourself down? Why is it so much easier to call myself ugly or stupid, than say I'm pretty or brilliant? self-love is something I'm still working on... I want to be easier on myself, and learn to praise myself more than put myself down. It should be easier than this, but it's something worth working for. someday, I know I'll be my own best friend... I'll just have to work for it.

hate

love

Artwork created by Caroline Ikeji

Caroline understands the struggle to accept herself just as she is, but knows it is a journey she is willing to take. On this page, she turned one photo upside down to visually communicate the idea of mixed feelings. Trials in our lives can be opportunities to discover who we really are. Don't be afraid to include personal journaling like Caroline's on a scrapbook page. It will reveal an authentic piece of who you are.

Supplies: Patterned paper (7gypsies, Scenic Route); letter stickers (American Crafts); label (Paper Source); stitching sticker (Sandylion); flower (Making Memories); adhesive (3L); Misc: brads

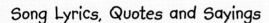

Song Lyrics, Quotes and Sayings

Stuck in a rut trying to think of the perfect title or journaling for your layout? Song lyrics can provide the perfect inspiration to get your layouts rockin' to a fresh beat. It's easy to capture a friend's personality with a song. Here's a list of songs that speak to the theme of friendship:

- **That's What Friends Are For** performed by Dionne Warwich & Friends
- **Wind Beneath My Wings** performed by Bette Midler
- **With a Little Help From My Friends** performed by The Beatles
- **Circle of Friends** performed by Point of Grace
- **Friends** performed by Michael W. Smith

- **You've Got a Friend in Me** performed by Randy Newman
- **Please Remember** performed by Leanne Rimes
- **Oh, How the Years Go By** performed by Amy Grant
- **My Best Friend** performed by Tim McGraw
- **Lean on Me** performed by Kirk Franklin

And don't forget that favorite quotes and poetry can also speak volumes when you're at a loss for words. Let the words of others perfectly encapsulate your feelings for a friend.

Kathleen knows the value of a "glass half full" mentality and learning to be your own best friend. Use a poem, quote or popular phrase to sum up an idea or feeling as she did here. When planning your layout, select colors, patterns and textures that reflect your own character and personality. For Kathleen, soft greens and pinks blend perfectly with floral accents to bring together a cohesive design alongside her portrait.

Supplies: Cardstock; patterned paper (BasicGrey, Daisy D's, My Mind's Eye); stamps (Inque Boutique); rhinestone brads (Making Memories); rickrack (SEI); Misc: ink, staple

Artwork created by Kathleen Summers

If you have nothing in life but a great friend, you're rich.
—Michelle Kwan

Chapter Four
Weekday COMPANIONS

When you think about your days, who is it that you spend the most time with? It's likely not your partner or your kids or your parents. The people you spend hours upon hours with in the course of your day, depending on your place in life, are your classmates or co-workers. Friendships forged in the walls of academia or around the water cooler at the office are ones grounded in a commonality, but they can grow to be much more. In this chapter, you'll find ways to chronicle the relationships fostered during the hours of the day. So turn the page to see some stunning examples of layouts featuring these amazing people who share the daily grind.

All in a Day's Work

Eight hours a day, five days a week, 250-plus days a year are spent at a job outside the home. Our coworkers see us day in and day out, sometimes for greater amounts of time than our kids, partners or parents. It is natural then that some great friendships grow out of our work relationships. These people share a common interest (whether that is the job itself or the acquisition of cash from said job), and when like minds come together, there are bound to be some good times.

Artwork created by Debi Boler

Seriously, some people have all the luck! Debi counts her job and her coworkers among her many blessings. She enjoys going to work with these people every day, and to celebrate these bonds she created this digital layout featuring each of their photographs. When creating work-related layouts, use items such as labels, staples and duct tape to support an office theme.

Supplies: Digital frame, label, paper, staples, tape, title letters by Katie Pertiet (Designer Digitals); patterned paper by Jesse Edwards (Designer Digitals); curled edge by Anna Aspnes (Designer Digitals); Misc: Pea Jenny Script font

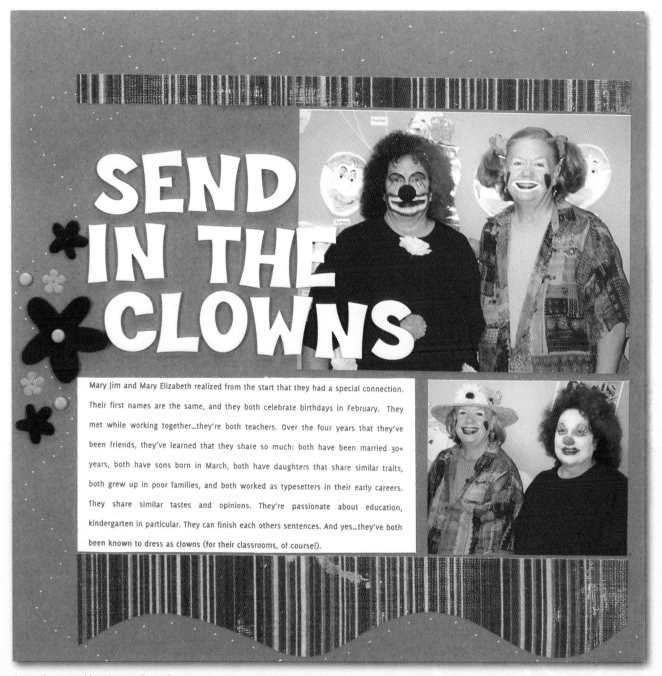

SEND IN THE CLOWNS

Mary Jim and Mary Elizabeth realized from the start that they had a special connection. Their first names are the same, and they both celebrate birthdays in February. They met while working together...they're both teachers. Over the four years that they've been friends, they've learned that they share so much: both have been married 30+ years, both have sons born in March, both have daughters that share similar traits, both grew up in poor families, and both worked as typesetters in their early careers. They share similar tastes and opinions. They're passionate about education, kindergarten in particular. They can finish each others sentences. And yes...they've both been known to dress as clowns (for their classrooms, of course!).

Artwork created by Katrina Simeck

These two teachers soon discovered that they not only share the same first name, but similar tastes and opinions (and apparently hairstyles and makeup too!). Katrina's colorful layout showcases photos of these two special ladies accompanied by coordinating patterned paper and dainty floral accents in teal and candy apple red. Foam letter stickers create a quick and easy title, and journaling printed in red completes the page.

Supplies: Cardstock; patterned paper (Daisy D's); letter stickers (Crafts Etc.); felt flowers (American Crafts); paper flowers (Prima); Misc: brads, pen

It's all about the O

Miss Opel ● Miss Ohneck ● Miss Opel

We're the English 12 team at Carroll High School. Three single girls working together to create a senior curriculum without rival. Can't get excited about Chaucer, Orwell, or Shakespeare? Look no further cuz these ladies are gonna rock your Brit. Lit. world! We've even collaboratively created a test that incorporates songs by Eminem, Martina McBride, and Led Zeppelin to teach literary analysis. Oh, yes. At CHS, English 12 is all about the O!

Artwork created by Susan Opel

This colorful page features three single girls working together to create an exciting learning environment for high school students. They make learning fun with music from artists such as Eminem and Led Zeppelin. The "O" theme is carried out on the left side of the page through the title, journaling, patterned paper and "O" accents. The right side is balanced with a striking oversized photo of the three photo subjects, and two small fabric flowers add to the girly tone.

Supplies: Cardstock; flowers, patterned paper, ribbon (Deja Views); Misc: Century Gothic and Invitation fonts

For **nine months** Kate was the one person I saw every single weekday.

We shared a crazy job that only the other one of us would understand.

It was just us in this tiny office.

Even though I was a year older, we had so much in common and lots to talk about.

Including both dating boys named Kevin, a shopping addiction, and love of GREY's.

After **nine months** Kate got smart and found a new job.

I knew when she told me she had an interview she'd get the position.

She was the most responsible, poised, personable girl I knew.

It was sad to see her go after we'd shared so much that year.

I cheered her on as she quit but was jealous she escaped first.

nine months

It was exactly **nine months** before I saw Kate again. So much had changed... I didn't even live in Chicago anymore. But it was great to sit down at one of our favorite restaurants and catch up. We had so much to talk about, especially new jobs that we both love. And retouched a friendship that means so much to me.

Artwork created by Kelly Purkey

Kelly and Kate both worked at a job that almost got the best of them. Despite the circumstances, they connected and remain dear friends to this day. The large title jumps right off the page and is further enhanced by two circular photographs in place of letters. Cut your journaling into strips for an easy way to break up text and select a patterned paper with preprinted words to support your theme. Add felt flowers and ribbon for a feminine touch.

Supplies: Cardstock; patterned paper (KI Memories); brads, buttons, flowers, ribbon (American Crafts); Misc: Impact and SP Strut fonts, circle cutter, paper punch

SWEET TOOTH

Yep... Jenny's got a serious sweet tooth. I've never met anyone who loves sweets more than she does. And, I've never worked with anyone who can tempt me more to indulge in the occasional (!) afternoon treat... which is tough when I'm trying to watch my weight! She can afford the extra calories... I can't! But, you know what? Ya gotta love this girl! She's the best coworker we've every had... which is really important when there are only three of us working in the office! And, hey... seriously... how can you not like someone who loves chocolate? Really?

Oct. '07

Artwork created by Debi Boler

Debi has the perfect coworker—she's fun to work with and always has chocolate on hand so her cubicle is a favorite stop on the way to the copier. On this digital layout Debi featured a portrait of her coworker accented by a circle of dots and mini brads. She added fun accents such as the stamped candy wrapper, pink mini brads and lollipop-colored patterned paper to support the candy theme.

Supplies: Digital brush, candy wrapper, date stamp, paper, ribbon by Katie Pertiet (Designer Digitals); Misc: SP Toby Type font

We have the hardest jobs in the whole world. We are stay-at-home moms. To keep each other sane, we do everything together on the phone - we do dishes, fold laundry, mop the floor, and even discipline the kids together while we're on the phone. She is the best colleague!

A WILL finds A WAY -Marden

the best
COLLEAGUE

HOUSE RULES DUE DATE ARRIVAL DATE HE SAID I SAID YOU SAID WELL DONE CLEAN UP GOOD TIMES HERE COMES TROUBLE THIS IS ONLY A

Artwork created by Stephanie Vetne

Even stay-at-home moms need someone to be their sounding board every now and then. Or a friend to just talk to while they are emptying the dishwasher. Stephanie pays homage to her favorite colleague with three oversized photos and handwritten journaling sharing all the day-to-day details of being a domestic engineer. Use a monochromatic color scheme like Stephanie did here with a combination of blues, and add a small punch of color in the form of multi-colored floral accents.

Supplies: Cardstock (WorldWin); patterned paper (K&Co., Sandylion); letter stickers (American Crafts, Arctic Frog); rub-ons (BasicGrey); stickers (7gypsies, Daisy D's); adhesive (3L); Misc: pen

School Friends

School. We all have to go whether we like it or not. It may be hard to believe, but some kids actually hate to miss school when they are sick because it is just too boring to stay home. There is never anything on TV that is as good as chasing boys on the playground or hearing the latest "who's going with whom" soap opera of high school. Some of these early friendships have stood the test of time for those of us who are long removed from the school years. So it makes sense to celebrate the ways in which these relationships have enriched our lives. It's likely your own offspring have cherished friends, classmates and teammates as well. In either case, there is a place in our scrapbooks for the circle of friends from school.

Artwork created by Caroline Ikeji

Caroline and Kate became fast friends in journalism class and soon they ruled the school! Select a mixture of bold patterned papers and layer them to create dimension and texture, as Caroline did here. Use the rule of thirds (see page 33 for definition) to divide your layout into three columns. Place floral embellishments in the left column, handwritten journaling and a title in the middle column and three candid photos stacked vertically in the right column.

Supplies: Cardstock (WorldWin); patterned paper (Hambly, K&Co., Scenic Route, Stemma); letter stickers (American Crafts, Chatterbox); buttons (Making Memories); stickers (Heidi Grace); decorative tape, tag (Stemma); adhesive (3L)

Artwork created by Nancy Jones

This layout perfectly captured the fun spontaneity that these two best friends share. Two photo booth strips of photos and an original handwritten class note give this page authenticity and a high school flair. The unique angles of the photographs and titling give this layout energy and movement. Use a mosaic of colorful patterned papers as a background to make the photos pop off the page.

Supplies: Cardstock; patterned paper, ribbon, stickers (Kl Memories); chipboard letters (Paper Studio)

tigers > Sydney and Deanna

two

They met on facebook girls looking for

Finding EACH otHer WAS the HARd PART. being instant Friends EASy!

Artwork created by Silvia Wainscott

These two girls have true school spirit. Silvia used a bold color palette to symbolize the team colors and the girls' exuberant personalities. Arrows draw the eye to the important journaling details while a large flower in the lower right corner grounds the layout. Wrap your title around a large focal photo to create a bold statement on your page. Print or handwrite any additional journaling tidbits on a hidden tag to allow for maximum use of visual elements like the oversized flower on the page background.

Supplies: Cardstock; patterned paper (Autumn Leaves, Dream Street); chipboard letters (BasicGrey); arrow accents (One Heart One Mind); rub-ons (American Crafts); Misc: buttons, ink, rickrack

They met on facebook, two girls looking for a roommate. They bonded over lunch at the mall. Now they take care of each other. They hang out together, watch Grey's anatomy, check out the frat boys, show support for the team! They have become more than just roommates. They are best friends!

...it's all about the friends. that's right. we chose this team because of the girls who would be your teammates. Sure, the club has a great reputation and the coaching is super, but for you, it's all about playing with friends... girls you actually like! And, this team is filled to the brim with that... you played All-Stars and APP with Courtney, Claire and Lauren and you play with them and Sophie at school. You played with Kelsey at the Strikers and you played with Natalie and Kat on the Lasers. As for the rest of the girls... Rachel, Heather, Dani, Amber, Elizabeth, Mary and Brooke... they are friends already! Yep... it's all about the friends this time! (2007-2008)

Artwork created by Debi Boler

Debi's daughter Shannon has been on various soccer teams in her young life, but finally decided she wanted to be a part of one that offered a wealth of good friendships in addition to an amazing track record. Debi kept this digital layout simple by arranging a visual triangle with her focal photo, two supporting photos and three digital flowers. Experiment with placing photographs and text in different places on your background for an eye-pleasing design.

Supplies: Digital flowers, frame, paper by Katie Pertiet (Designer Digitals); title letters by Jesse Edwards (Designer Digitals); tissue paper by Anna Aspnes (Designer Digitals); brads by Pattie Knox (Designer Digitals); Misc: Pea Cassie font

it was so hard for you to go away
for the week of outdoor science
school. you really are a homebody
and you were afraid you'd miss me.
which you actually did. but the fact
that you were away from home with
all your friends made the week just
a bit (?) more tolerable. the excitement
of this first morning filled the air with
laughter, giggles and lots of smiles!
once you were at camp, you later
told me you missed me terribly but
you loved having your best friends
bunking right beside you. it's not
easy to replace your mom, but
your friends come close, right?
october 2005

mariners elementary · outdoor science school, san bernardino mountains

Artwork created by Debi Boler

Outdoor science school was a wonderful (albeit scary) week of learning and bunking with best friends. It was great that all the girls were there for each other, especially for those moments when they were a little homesick. To chronicle their adventure, Debi created this digital layout in beige and army green for an outdoor feel. Green mini brads and three strips of camouflage patterned paper support the theme while a collection of photos and paragraph-style journaling tell the story.

Supplies: Digital papers, string tie by Katie Pertiet (Designer Digitals); title letters by Lynn Grieveson (Designer Digitals); brads by Pattie Knox (Designer Digitals)

Four years ago Kent and Kurt played on their first soccer team. Kurt was shy and reluctant; Kent was awkward, but energetic. Their teammates were friends they had known since they were 2 years old. Fast forward those four years and you'll find that same group of friends, boys and girls, as classmates, soccer teammates, and baseball teammates. They spend many weekends together not only playing sports, but also playing at each other's houses. Each year before school starts, all of them are anxious to see which of their friends are in their class that year. There is always one or two. I have no doubt that in a few more years; you'll still find this group of friends hanging out together. Or maybe...even dating! Now wouldn't that be something!

Artwork created by Mary Larson

Mary's twin boys have been playing soccer and baseball with the same core group of kids for the past four years. She expects they will continue to be friends for a long time to come and maybe even date someday! In the meantime, she has fun documenting their good times in scrapbook pages like this one. Use large chipboard letters for a bold title wrapped around a montage of action photos. A graph-style transparency background works well for sport-theme layouts and chipboard stars are the perfect embellishments to accent star players, no matter the sport.

Supplies: Cardstock (WorldWin); patterned transparency (Hambly); chipboard letters (Maya Road); brads (Provo Craft); adhesive (3L); Misc: chipboard stars and word, ink

Artwork created by Karen Shand

These two sweet girls have been friends since kindergarten. Their tried-and-true friendship even connected their moms who are now friends and scrapbooking buddies. Karen used a sunny color palette of yellow and blue and added a garden of flowers to give this page a girly charm. Add visual interest to a traditional strip of photos by cropping the images with a curve to lead the eye along the page. Trim a block of patterned paper with a scalloped border and stamp dates on mini paper flowers for a soft touch.

Supplies: Cardstock; patterned paper (American Crafts); chipboard letters, transparent flowers (Heidi Swapp); flowers (Hobby Lobby, Prima); stamps (JustRite, Making Memories); Misc: Benguit Frisky font, brads, mesh

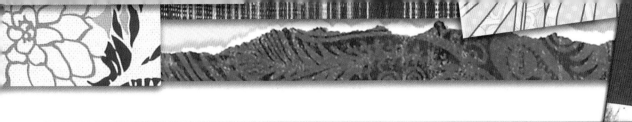

Artwork created by Mary Russo

Mary received a piece of artwork created by her son Christopher's best friend Petey. Mary scanned the drawing to include it on this endearing scrapbook page showcasing these two best buds and then gave the creation to Petey as an unexpected gift. Children's artwork can be one of the best features to add to a scrapbook layout. It lends authenticity and is a perfect way to preserve a treasured piece of art.

Supplies: Cardstock; patterned paper (K&Co., Karen Foster); chipboard letters (Scenic Route); stickers (K&Co.); Misc: brads, ink

A true friend is one who thinks you are a
good egg even if you are half-cracked.

—Author unknown

Chapter Five

YOU'VE GOT A Friend IN ME

Cross my heart and hope to die, stick a needle in my eye. As kids we would pinky swear, cross our hearts, and even took the pledge that we would rather risk blindness by a sharp sewing object than to share a secret. No matter what our age may be, we all need someone in our lives with whom we can share our innermost thoughts and feelings and lean on for support. This section features a few pages about those special friends who touch our hearts in ways we never thought possible. The kindred spirits who always laugh at our jokes no matter how lame, offer a shoulder to cry on and never mind if we call at 4 a.m. These are the ones who truly deserve a place in our scrapbooks so we may cherish the joy and companionship they bring to our lives.

The Vault

Whatever what your age, a very important characteristic of cherished friend is the ability to keep a secret. No matter how juicy it is. Kitty calls her secret-keeping friend The Vault: secrets go in but they don't come out. You needn't record all your secrets in your scrapbooks, but do make room on your pages for your relationships with your closest confidants.

Artwork created by Deena Wuest

Deena captured her daughter and her best friend telling "boy" secrets. It's a classic rite of passage for girls, and these two seem to be getting a head start! If you lean toward a graphic style, the design of this digital page may be for you. Deena kept her page clean and crisp by featuring artistic photography, simple journaling and an image of a merchandise SKU. Look to print ads and other media for inspiration when creating graphic pages like this one.

Supplies: Software (Adobe); digital brush and paper by Katie Pertiet (Designer Digitals); friend brush by Mary Ann Wise (Designer Digitals); Misc: Avant Garde and Rage Italic fonts

Artwork created by Wendy McKeehan

These little girls are not quite ready for secrets—they talk too loud and always turn right around and tell the secret to someone else. But that didn't stop Wendy from showing just how cute they are. This digital page contains layers of patterned papers set at different angles to keep the reader's eye moving across the page. Use big, bold white letters to deliver a title with impact and add a few circles and other accents for an eye-pleasing page.

Supplies: Digital paper, page kit by Anna Aspnes (Designer Digitals); brush frame, journaling tag, notebook paper by Katie Pertiet (Designer Digitals); ribbon by Lynn Grieveson (Designer Digitals)

SECRETS

What can I say? It's not decent or ladylike, but I can't help myself... I love SKINNYDIPPING. Every Thursday night my roommates and I would pile into my car and head to 1st Dam. We stood together on the shore, stripped off our clothes, counted to 3 and threw ourselves into the icy cold waters. Our screams and squeals filled the night air. It was our ritual every week. I started it and I loved every minute of it. Am I ashamed of my secret? No, but I'm not going to put it on my resume either.

shy?

Artwork created by Emilie Ahern

There's nothing quite like a night of skinny dipping to bond a group of college roommates. Emilie created this great page to document their crazy friendship and top-secret (until now!) ritual. She kept her background free of heavy embellishments and made good use of white space at the top of her page. Place a photo and title letters at a slight tilt to add rhythm to a clean layout like this one. Machine-stitch patterned papers and add metal accents for a bit of shine.

Supplies: Cardstock; patterned paper (My Mind's Eye); chipboard letters, rub-ons (Cosmo Cricket); flower brads (Nunn Design)

Being the daughter of a
military man isn't
exactly easy I bet. I guess that's why I'm glad
that you love school so much.
It's been your life. Not only
because you love the
actual school work, but
because it's been your only way to make friends
between

each duty station. It's so great
to see you bond with other
kids your age so well such as
Ali. The two of you are like
little peas in a pod.
Someday soon we will move
again but you will always
have this friendship
as well as many, many
others to remember
in your lifetime.

BE TRUE TO YOURSELF

Artwork created by Mandy Koontz

As a military kid, it can be a challenge to make new friends when moving from one duty station to another. Mandy is grateful her daughter loves school and has an easy time developing friendships at each new one she attends. This digital layout composed in rich raspberry hues contains a bouquet of flowers and hearts dispersed around a block of journaling and a cheery photo. Experiment with arranging digital elements atop a colorful background to add movement and energy to your page.

Supplies: Digital cardstock by Bren Boone (Scrapbook Graphics); swirls by Anne DeJong (Funky Playground); page kits by Jackie Eckles and Jomi van Bekkum (ScrapArtist) and Kate Hadfield, Michelle Godin and Rachel Young (Funky Playground); tiny flowers by Kate Hadfield (Lilypad); ribbons, strings by Natalie Braxton (Lilypad); flower layers (Ah Designs); dot brush by Michelle Coleman (Little Dreamer); overlay by Christina Renee (Funky Playground); embellishments (Sweet Shoppe Designs); Misc: Pea Breathe Easy font

Journaling

When it comes to journaling, there are many methods you can employ to document the story or emotion behind a page. One way is to journal from the point of view of the photo subject(s). By writing in his or her voice, you reflect his or her inner persona or character. Here are some other fun ideas to keep in mind when journaling.

- Lists (bullets or numbered)
- Definitions
- Compare/Contrast
- Favorites
- Five Senses
- Then & Now
- Turning Point
- Who, What, When, Where, Why & How

Artwork created by Shannan Browning

Shannan and Kitty have been friends for more than a decade and have developed a jargon all their own. One will start to say something and the other will finish. Document special words or phrases you and a friend say while conversing. It will be fun to get them down in written form and the layout will serve as a memorable keepsake for years to come so you can remember all the quips and quotes that were so unique to that time in your life.

Supplies: Cardstock; stamps (Technique Tuesday); Misc: Gigi font, ink

94

It started before Kindergarten and as the years passed, your friendship with Maura continued to grow. It wasn't until the summer before second grade that we found out that Maura and her family were being transferred to California. This past year, the two of you have held onto that friendship via phone calls, letters and even a surprise visit for your birthday. I am proud of your dedication to this friendship that has thrived beyond the miles.

BEYOND the miles

Artwork created by Lisa Dorsey

These two cuties were separated when one of them had to move away, but they keep in touch on the phone and visit each other when they can. Lisa did a great job recording their friendship in this hip and happening layout full of girlish charm. By strategically arranging the photos, title and paper flowers, she created a visual triangle that moves the eye across the page. Adhere tiny rhinestones to the center of flowers and velvet ribbon to serve as stems. Not only will these elements create visual appeal, they will also add a little bit of dimension and soft texture.

Supplies: Cardstock; patterned paper (American Crafts, Creative Imaginations, Reminisce); letter stickers (American Crafts, Making Memories); ribbon (Fancy Pants); rhinestones (Westrim)

A Friend to Lean On

There are times when we all need a hand. Sometimes we are the ones giving support and other times we are on the receiving end. Support can come in many ways such as prayer, encouragement or just being a shoulder to cry on. These acts of support, whether big or small, should be recorded in our scrapbooks. For these are the things that make us smile, make us cry and remind us that we are loved by others.

Artwork created by Kimber McGray

Kimber was caught off guard by the unexpected kindness from a new friend. She instantly took a picture of the precious gift and recorded the story in a scrapbook page. She left a generous amount of white space surrounding the photo block to lend an open and airy feel. A pretty palette of pinks mixed with a bit of fresh green keeps the page soft and feminine.

Supplies: Cardstock (WorldWin); patterned paper (Anna Griffin, We R Memory Keepers); letter stickers (American Crafts); stickers (Creative Imaginations); die-cut accent (Sassafras Lass); ribbon (Offray); photo corners (Heidi Swapp); adhesive (3L); Misc: office clip, vellum

pray...

"Be joyful in hope, patient in affliction, faithful in prayer." Romans 12:12

Without Ceasing

Bernie and I have been prayer warriors for one another for years. Both of us have had surgeries and trials, she far greater than I. Despite it all, her faith is strong and sustaining, and I pray for her daily. On this last trip to the hospital, however, I despaired that my beloved friend would not pull through. I prayed without ceasing, and was so blessed the day she was strong enough for my visit. As I held her frail hand, I was so grateful that God had answered my prayer, and we could pray together once more.

Artwork created by Rita Shimniok

In addition to the opportunity for artistic expression, scrapbooking allows us to articulate our deepest feelings. On this page, Rita honors her dear friend and prayer warrior Bernie. Her journaling is filled with emotion and gratitude for having been so blessed to have this beloved friend in her life. Allow your feelings to flow when composing your journaling, and don't hold anything back. Include a befitting Bible verse or quote and place a touching photo front and center.

Supplies: Cardstock; chipboard letters and accents, die-cut letters, patterned paper (BasicGrey); paper flowers (Prima); Misc: Clarendon, Jayne Print and Papyrus fonts, brads, buttons, ink, paint

Artwork created by Carolyn McAfee

Throughout the years, Carolyn has always known she could count on her sister. She pays tribute to their unbreakable bond with this contemporary page filled with repeating floral and circular elements. If you'd like to include a variety of photos from different time periods, a good bet is to convert them to black and white to keep the colors and backgrounds from clashing. Keep the most recent image in color, and pull hues from within it when selecting paper and embellishments. Trim a large circle to frame the focal photo and place the letters to follow the circle's arch.

Supplies: Patterned paper (Around the Block, KI Memories, NRN, Sandylion); patterned transparency (KI Memories); chipboard letters and accents (Deluxe Designs, Heidi Swapp); journaling accents (Heidi Swapp); brads, flowers (Queen & Co.)

when i need to talk about shoes, or possible haircuts, or celebrities, or our boys, or being a mom, or the new John Mayer album, or trips to New York city, or the incredible sale at J Crew (or baby gap) or Rick & bubba, or crows feet, or designer jeans, or Dancing with the stars, or anything else totally girly or seriously silly

I have these girls

Karly, Me & Leah 6·24·07

Artwork created by Katie Brunett

There are three forms of communication: telegraph, telephone and tell-a-woman! Whether it's a good sale at their favorite clothing store or the latest gossip on a hunky celebrity, Katie and her friends tell each other everything. These three are definitely in the know! If the photo you would like to feature is a bit blurred, desaturate it using image-editing software and add a grungy frame around the edges for a dreamy effect. Punch a variety of patterned papers into circles and arrange in a downward slope to draw the eye to focal point of the page. Letter stickers work great for an easy title.

Supplies: Cardstock; flowers, letter stickers, patterned paper (American Crafts); charm (7gypsies); digital frame by Rhonna Farrer (Two Peas in a Bucket); Misc: brads, colored pencils

She is my SUPERHERO

able to leap tall buildings in a single bound....er, scratch that...

take excellent photos of tall buildings with a single click!

she is faster than a speeding bullet...when it comes to making awesome pages!

Look up in the sky! It's a bird, it's a plane...... NO! It's Kimber McGray!

Scrapbook extraordinaire, keeper of my secrets and the most amazing friend!

She may look faceless here (all great superhero's have their secret identity, don't ya know) but her face is very familiar to me. It's one I see almost everyday. While I don't actually see it in person, we send instant messages to each other and view a tiny little avatar photo of each other while we chat about our daily lives. We share just about everything with each other and I've even met her kids and she has met mine. She is someone that I admire and adore but more than that, I think she makes it all worthwhile when I can share my success with someone who has the outstanding power to make me feel great.

Two of us at CHA-Chicago '07

Artwork created by Sherry Steveson

Every superhero hides his or her identity behind a mask or disguise, but in this case, it's a camera! Sherry's friend Kimber is her hero for many reasons, and she shows just how much she admires her friend's amazing photography skills in this two-page spread. Print large photos to span across the gutter and border them with long strips of patterned papers. For a little sparkle and shine, add glitter glue to oversized chipboard letters. If you want to get a little touchy-feely, adhere felt letters and mini paper flowers to add a bit of texture and dimension.

Supplies: Cardstock; patterned paper (Doodlebug, KI Memories); chipboard letters (Everlasting Keepsakes); letter stickers (American Crafts); flowers (Prima); Misc: brads, dimensional glaze, paint

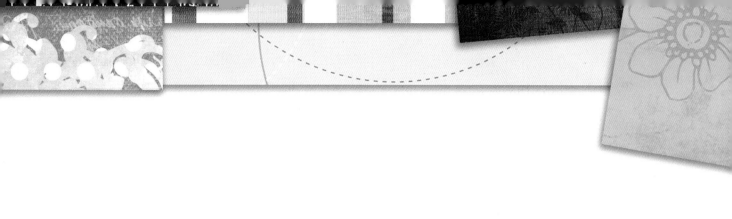

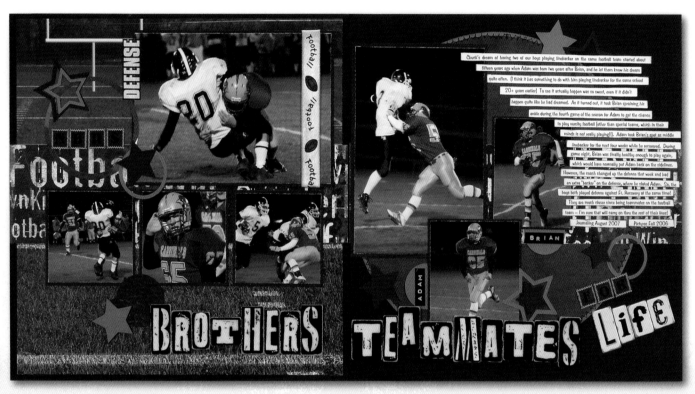

Artwork created by Karen Shand

On this memorable night, a father's dream came true: both of his sons played defense at the same time! Karen decided to dedicate a two-page layout celebrating the bond forged between these two brothers and their love of the sport. She included a bonanza of football-related paper and embellishments, but it's the collage of action photos that steal the limelight on this stunner of a scrapbook page. Add urban-style letters for a manly title treatment and print journaling onto strips to tell your story. Include additional shapes like stars and circles to add even more color and pop to the page.

Supplies: Cardstock; patterned paper (Scrappin' Sports); chipboard letters (Li'l Davis); labels (Dymo); die-cut shapes (Provo Craft); ribbon (Paper Studio); Misc: Benguit Frisky font, ink

i love you, girls.

imagine what life would be like if we could be together all the time.

imagine the laughter.

i don't like missing moments in your lives but, i know you think of me when i am not there.

(you guys took this photo at Caylee's baby shower, May 2007... thanks for thinking of me)

Artwork created by Carrie Postma

This photo is better than the standard "wish you were here" postcard friends mail you from vacation. In this case, it really is the next best thing to being there. Carrie was so touched by the photo her friends sent her she just knew she had to put it to good use on a scrapbook page. A clean, white background is accented with a flourish of floral embellishments that add a girly touch. The supporting photo placed at an angle and the large green arrow draw the eye to the focal point.

Supplies: Cardstock; chipboard letters and accents (Deluxe Designs, Fancy Pants, Making Memories); acrylic letters, rub-ons (Heidi Swapp); rhinestone accents (Heidi Swapp, Making Memories); flowers (Making Memories); Misc: paint

Artwork created by Jennifer Emch

Jennifer knows how blessed she is to not only find one person that is special...but two! She chronicles the story of their friendship in handwritten journaling. A large photo of all three women balances the left side while a floral embellishment serves as an eye-pleasing accent. Tear patterned paper to create a distressed feel and add word stickers to support your theme.

Supplies: Cardstock; patterned paper (American Crafts, My Mind's Eye, Paper Wishes); stickers (7gypsies); stamps (Catslife Press); Misc: ink

You're My Best Friend

We all have dear friends that mean the world to us. These comrades brighten our days, help us through the rough parts and always laugh at our jokes whether they are funny or not. They inspire us to try new things, always include us in their plans and are only just a phone call away if we need them. These are the people we can't imagine our life without. So create layouts to express in words what these people mean in your heart.

Artwork created by Kitty Foster

Kitty pays tribute to her good friend Shannan in this sweet layout expressing the value of honesty in friendship. An oversized black-and-white photo takes center stage and is only accented with a frame of candy-apple hearts and polka-dot ribbon. Use a simple block of handwritten journaling to express your deepest sentiments to a cherished friend. Leave the remainder of your background free of heavy embellishments to keep it clean and simple and to allow your photo to shine.

Supplies: Patterned paper (Daisy D's); stamps (Inque Boutique); adhesive (3L); Misc: 2Peas Sailboat font, ink, ribbon

K&J

Ah, my friend Kathy Rietsema. We have been friends since 1990. As a foursome we have traveled to Europe (more than once), Egypt and Costa Rica together. We have also taken lots of shorter trips in the U.S. Unfortunately for us, the Ritsemas moved to Grand Rapids about 5 years ago to be nearer to their children and grandchildren, so we seldom see them anymore. What is special about Kathy (and what we miss most) is that she would call us up on a Friday or Saturday and ask us to go to a movie or a play or a restaurant and we would drop everything and GO! She was our activity director for sure. One of my fondest memories is of Kathy and me sitting in Lake Michigan and giggling as the waves rolled over us. As you can see, it did not take much to get us going. The guys did not think it was THAT funny. Go figure.

-Jean
journaled 1/07, photo 8/05

Artwork created by Wendy McKeehan

These two have traveled the world together, hung out on the beaches of Lake Michigan and celebrated milestone anniversaries and birthdays together. It is a friendship for the ages. Chocolate brown works as a great mixer to accent soft pinks and greens. Use monogram initials in place of spelling out the full names of your photo subjects. Add paisleys, florals and swirls for a feminine flair.

Supplies: Cardstock (WorldWin); patterned paper (Imagination Project); chipboard letters (Maya Road); chipboard accent (Magistical Memories); rub-ons (BasicGrey); stained glass spray paint (Krylon); ribbon (Maya Road); adhesive (3L); Misc: Century Gothic font

Artwork created by Wendy McKeehan

In honor of Ken's 50th birthday (and one whale of a party), Wendy paid tribute to her friend with a commemorative page she will give to him housed in a frame. She mixed a graph-paper transparency background and mini file folder labels with sparkly numbers and shiny buttons for a unique juxtaposition. Birthday pages are great for showcasing a large photo of the guest of honor. Print computer-generated journaling over a photo for an interesting visual element.

Supplies: Cardstock (WorldWin); patterned paper (Creative Imaginations); patterned transparency (Hambly); letter stickers (Making Memories); chipboard letters (Heidi Swapp); chipboard numbers (Maya Road); buttons (Autumn Leaves); stamp (Inque Boutique); adhesive (3L); Misc: Century Gothic font, buttons, embossing powder

Artwork created by Cindy Tobey

Cindy and her friend Amy are knitted together by the same beliefs, hobbies and love of coffee. Cindy even included some yarn from her friend's favorite fiber company to show just how much she values this special friendship. A knitting needle, buttons and thread woven through punched circles in cardstock further support the crafty theme. If there is a hobby your friend is in love with, illustrate her passion for it by featuring a close-up shot of her happily engaged in the activity.

Supplies: Patterned paper, chipboard letters, metal bookplate, ribbon (We R Memory Keepers); rub-on letters (Autumn Leaves, K&Co.); lace (Rusty Pickle); buttons (Autumn Leaves, We R Memory Keepers); Misc: Script Hand font, ink, paint

In Tribute

At some point in our lives we will lose a friend and having memories of them in our books will become even more important after they are gone. Whether it is a page of thanks for what a friend has taught you or one with sweet reminders after their passing, archiving these memories in our scrapbooks is a wonderful way to record and share these memories with others.

Artwork created by Shannan Browning

Shannan created this page in loving memory of her dear friend Jennifer. It was important for Shannan to record her thoughts of her dear friend who left this world too soon. Fill the left side of your page with a block of journaling sharing special details of the person you are honoring. Balance the right side with an endearing focal photo and a block of patterned paper with plenty of white space. Ground your layout with a title created from large handpainted chipboard letters.

Supplies: Patterned paper (My Mind's Eye); chipboard letters (FTI, KI Memories); acrylic letters (Heidi Swapp); rub-on words (KI Memories); rub-on letters (Imagination Project)

Pat and Royana at Nikki's wedding - October 1999

Royana Schultz
August 7, 1943 - December 26, 2001

Wish You Were Here

LOVED
YOU ARE LOVED

Artwork created by Wendy McKeehan

This digital page featuring Wendy's mom and paying tribute to her dear friend Royana is sure to tug at your heart-strings. The eye-popping red and cool turquoise colors perfectly blend with an artistic array of digital brushes and swirls. When paying tribute to someone you've lost, you may have an abundance of things you'd like to say in your journaling. In that case, try printing your text in a small, scripty font to fit everything in and to create a warm feel.

Supplies: Digital paper by Anna Aspnes and Dana Zarling (Designer Digitals); brushes by Anna Aspnes (Designer Digitals); frames by Anna Aspnes and Katie Pertiet (Designer Digitals); border, journal card by Katie Pertiet (Designer Digitals); Misc: Century Gothic and Rage Italic fonts

source guide

The following companies manufacture products featured in this book. Please check your local retailers to find these materials, or go to a company's Web site for the latest product. In addition, we have made every attempt to properly credit the items mentioned in this book. We apologize to any company that we have listed incorrectly, and we would appreciate hearing from you.

3L Corporation—Scrapbook Adhesives
(800) 828-3130
www.scrapbook-adhesives.com

7gypsies
(877) 749-7797
www.sevengypsies.com

AccuCut
(800) 288-1670
www.accucut.com

Adobe Systems Incorporated
(800) 833-6687
www.adobe.com

Adornit/Carolee's Creations
(435) 563-1100
www.adornit.com

Adrienne Looman
www.aloomanart.com

Ah! Designs
www.amyhutchinsondesigns.com

American Crafts
(801) 226-0747
www.americancrafts.com

Anna Griffin, Inc.
(888) 817-8170
www.annagriffin.com

Arctic Frog
(479) 636-3764
www.arcticfrog.com

Around The Block
(801) 593-1946
www.aroundtheblockproducts.com

Autumn Leaves
(800) 588-6707
www.autumnleaves.com

BasicGrey
(801) 544-1116
www.basicgrey.com

Bazzill Basics Paper
(480) 558-8557
www.bazzillbasics.com

Berwick Offray, LLC
(800) 344-5533
www.offray.com

Blumenthal Lansing Company
(563) 538-4211
www.buttonsplus.com

Catslife Press
(541) 902-7855
www.harborside.com/~catslife/

Chatterbox, Inc.
(888) 416-6260
www.chatterboxinc.com

CherryArte
(212) 465-3495
www.cherryarte.com

Christina Renee Designs
www.christinareneedesigns.com

Color It
(800) 833-6687
www.adobe.com

Cosmo Cricket
(800) 852-8810
www.cosmocricket.com

Crafts, Etc. Ltd.
(800) 888-0321 x 1275
www.craftsetc.com

Crate Paper
(801) 798-8996
www.cratepaper.com

Creative Imaginations
(800) 942-6487
www.cigift.com

Daisy D's Paper Company
(888) 601-8955
www.daisydspaper.com

Deflect-O Corporation
(800) 428-4328
www.deflecto.com

Dèjà Views
(800) 243-8419
www.dejaviews.com

Deluxe Designs
(480) 497-9005
www.deluxecuts.com

Designer Digitals
www.designerdigitals.com

Die Cuts With A View
(801) 224-6766
www.diecutswithaview.com

Doodlebug Design Inc.
(877) 800-9190
www.doodlebug.ws

Dream Street Papers
(480) 275-9736
www.dreamstreetpapers.com

Dymo
(800) 426-7827
www.dymo.com

EK Success, Ltd.
(800) 524-1349
www.eksuccess.com

Everlasting Keepsakes
(816) 896-7037
www.everlastingkeepsakes.com

Fancy Pants Designs, LLC
(801) 779-3212
www.fancypantsdesigns.com

FTI - Finishing Touch Ideas
www.finishingtouchideas.com.au

Funky Playground Designs
www.funkyplaygrounddesigns.com

Hambly Studios
(800) 451-3999
www.hamblystudios.com

Heidi Grace Designs, Inc.
(866) 348-5661
www.heidigrace.com

Heidi Swapp/Advantus Corporation
(904) 482-0092
www.heidiswapp.com

Hero Arts Rubber Stamps, Inc.
(800) 822-4376
www.heroarts.com

Hobby Lobby Stores, Inc.
www.hobbylobby.com

Hot Off The Press, Inc.
(800) 227-9595
www.b2b.hotp.com

Imagination Project, Inc.
(888) 477-6532
www.imaginationproject.com

Inque Boutique Inc.
www.goinque.com

Jenni Bowlin
www.jennibowlin.com

Junkitz - no longer in business

JustRite Stampers/Millenium Marking Company
(800) 545-7084
www.justritestampers.com

K&Company
(888) 244-2083
www.kandcompany.com

Karen Foster Design
(801) 451-9779
www.karenfosterdesign.com

Kevin and Amanda
www.kevinandamanda.com

KI Memories
(972) 243-5595
www.kimemories.com

Krylon
(800) 457-9566
www.krylon.com

Li'l Davis Designs
(480) 223-0080
www.lildavisdesigns.com

LilyPad, The
www.the-lilypad.com

Little Dreamer Designs
www.littledreamerdesigns.com

Magistical Memories
(818) 842-1540
www.magisticalmemories.com

Making Memories
(801) 294-0430
www.makingmemories.com

May Arts
(800) 442-3950
www.mayarts.com

Maya Road, LLC
(214) 488-3279
www.mayaroad.com

Me & My Big Ideas
(949) 583-2065
www.meandmybigideas.com

Mustard Moon
(763) 493-5157
www.mustardmoon.com

My Mind's Eye, Inc.
(800) 665-5116
www.mymindseye.com

NRN Designs
(888) 678-2734
www.nrndesigns.com

Nunn Design
(800) 761-3557
www.nunndesign.com

Offray- see Berwick Offray, LLC

One Bored Girl
www.oneboredgirl.etsy.com

One Heart...One Mind, LLC
(888) 414-3690
Oscraps
www.oscraps.com

Paper Source
(888) 727-3711
www.paper-source.com

Paper Studio
(480) 557-5700
www.paperstudio.com

Paper Trunk
(503) 855-3323
www.papertrunk.com

Paper Wishes by Hot Off the Press
(888) 300-3406
www.paperwishes.com

Petaloo
(800) 458-0350
www.petaloo.com

Pink Martini Designs - no longer in business

Polar Bear Press
(801) 451-7670
www.polarbearpress.com

Prima Marketing, Inc.
(909) 627-5532
www.primamarketinginc.com

Provo Craft
(800) 937-7686
www.provocraft.com

Queen & Co.
(858) 613-7858
www.queenandcompany.com

Reminisce Papers
(319) 358-9777
www.shopreminisce.com

Rusty Pickle
(801) 746-1045
www.rustypickle.com

Sandylion Sticker Designs
(800) 387-4215
www.sandylion.com

Sassafras Lass
(801) 269-1331
www.sassafraslass.com

Scenic Route Paper Co.
(801) 542-8071
www.scenicroutepaper.com

ScrapArtist
(734) 717-7775
www.scrapartist.com

Scrapbook Graphics
www.scrapbookgraphics.com

Scrappin' Sports & More
(877) 245-6044
www.scrappinsports.com

Scrapsupply
(615) 777-3953
www.scrapsupply.com

Scrapworks, LLC /
As You Wish Products, LLC
(801) 363-1010
www.scrapworks.com

SEI, Inc.
(800) 333-3279
www.shopsei.com

Shabby Princess
www.shabbyprincess.com

Sizzix
(877) 355-4766
www.sizzix.com

Stemma/Masterpiece Studios
www.masterpiecestudios.com

Sweet Shoppe Designs
www.sweetshoppedesigns.com

Target
www.target.com

Technique Tuesday, LLC
(503) 644-4073
www.techniquetuesday.com

Two Peas in a Bucket
(888) 896-7327
www.twopeasinabucket.com

Urban Lily
www.urbanlily.com

We R Memory Keepers, Inc.
(801) 539-5000
www.weronthenet.com

Weeds and Wildflowers Designs
www.weedsandwildflowersdesigns.com/shoppe

Westrim Crafts
(800) 727-2727
www.westrimcrafts.com

WorldWin Papers
(888) 834-6455
www.worldwinpapers.com

Index

Discover more inspiration and ideas with these titles from Memory Makers!

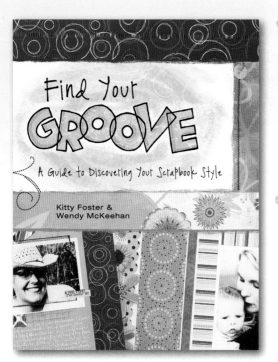

Find Your Groove

Kitty Foster and Wendy McKeehan take you on a journey to discovering your own groovy scrapbook style through quizzes, exercises, challenges and page after page of fabulous layouts sure to inspire.

ISBN-13: 978-1-59963-006-9
ISBN-10: 1-59963-006-0
Paperback
112 pages
Z0787

601 Great Scrapbook Ideas

Brimming with inspiration and ideas, you'll discover one amazing page after another in this big book of layouts.

ISBN-13: 978-1-59963-017-5
ISBN-10: 1-59963-017-6
Paperback
272 pages
Z1640

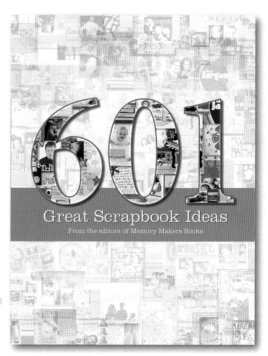

That's Life

Popular scrapbook designer Nic Howard shows how to identify, capture and chronicle everyday moments and daily routines in your scrapbook pages.

ISBN-13: 978-1-59963-001-4
ISBN-10: 1-59963-001-X
paperback
112 pages
Z0689

These books and other fine Memory Makers titles are available at your local scrapbook or craft store, bookstore or from online suppliers. Or visit us on the Web at www.memorymakers.com and www.mycraftivity.com.